WASHINGTON'S BEST LAKE FLY FISHING

Nathan Caproni

Frank Amato

PORTLAND

To my parents, Ken and Darlene, who inspired
me with the idea for this book. Their sacrifice,
encouragement, and help made it all possible.

Acknowledgments

Special thanks to my uncle and fishing partner, Bill Berg, and fishing partner,
Fritz Jorg, for introducing me years ago to the wonderful sport of fly fishing. Their
suggestions and encouragement were valuable in the process of writing this book.

I want to thank Department of Fisheries biologists, John Hisata, Kurt Vail, Bob
Peck, Joe Foster, Chuck Phillips, Jim Johnston, and Dan Collins for providing helpful
management information. Stocking data was provided by the Department of
Fisheries. Thanks to Terry Jackson for her effort in generating this stocking data.

And above all, thanks to God, The Creator, to whom I owe everything.

All photographs were taken by the author on Fujichrome transparency film
with a Nikon F-3 camera and Nikkor lenses from 24mm to 300mm. Whenever phys-
ically possible the camera was mounted on a sturdy Gitzo 320 tripod with a Studio
Ball tripod head. Mike Kirk quick release plates were used on the camera body and
lens tripod collars for use with the tripod head. The camera's internal mirror was
locked up at slower shutter speeds to maintain all possible sharpness. Polarizing
and warming filters were used occasionally.

Published in 1995 by Frank Amato Publications, Inc.
P.O. Box 82112, Portland, Oregon 97282
(503) 653-8108
ISBN: 1-57188-027-5
UPC: 0-66066-00215-0
Book Design: Charlie Clifford
Printed in Canada
1 3 5 7 9 10 8 6 4 2

Contents

Introduction

Treasure in Our Backyard

As the sun slowly disappeared behind the ridge, the crisp autumn air greedily absorbed the last of its warming rays. Nature had issued its decree—the season of life-giving warmth was finished. The endless struggle of seasons was manifest, autumn and winter demanding the attention of all observers. While the fading light played its entrancing game on the water, a large rainbow trout gorged itself in the shallows, sensing autumn's inevitable surrender.

Amid this unfolding scene in nature's drama, I quietly eased my float tube into position, every sense alert for the stalk. The oversized fish was "gulping" in a loud, unrestrained manner as it sucked insects from the surface film with fin and tail exposed. It was a beautiful thing to watch. The climax was reached as my line unrolled in the air, delicately delivering the fly to the edge of the riseform. After a few seconds I began my retrieve with two short line strips, and then . . . suddenly the rainbow struck the mini-leech pattern, exploding high out of the water no more than 20 feet away! After a series of strong runs and rod-jolting head shakes, the big rainbow finally gave in to the rod's steady pressure. What a fish! The 7-pound Washington rainbow was larger than I anticipated and certainly a highlight of the year.

Washington state offers some of the finest lake fishing for trout in the country. Not only is this in terms of the size, variety, and quality of fish, but also the great beauty and contrast of geography surrounding the lakes.

Anyone traveling in Washington state, taking part in its outdoor activities, or studying its many maps cannot help but notice an abundance of fresh water, lakes in particular. There are about 8,000 lakes, both natural and man-made, in a tremendous diversity of climate, vegetation, and terrain from near sea level to alpine elevations. These gems of nature are one of Washington's most invaluable resources.

What Does This Book Cover?

This book is designed to highlight the most productive trout lakes for fly fishing in each region of the state, guiding the angler and giving a good knowledge of each lake and what it offers. A productive lake, for most of the regional listings in this book, is one consistently producing large, healthy trout. This is due to either quality fish management, or an abundance of key nutrients and organisms essential to biological productivity—most often both together are required. As a rule of thumb, lakes receiving angler pressure depend on these criteria to produce numbers of large trout. Because of western Washington's typically less-productive lakes (Regions 4, 5, and 6) and slower-growing fish, strategic management and low fish harvest become especially important for large fish production.

The lake descriptions in this book are grouped into regional sections corresponding for the most part with Washington State Department of Fish and Wildlife management jurisdiction areas. Each lake description will contain information such as location and access, physical characteristics, management, fish sizes and species, history, and other items unique to each lake. When possible, I have included a bathymetric map, which outlines a lake's shape and shows a series of depth contours. I find these maps to be a very helpful tool, providing a foundation for the process of reading a lake and becoming intimately familiar with it. Reading a lake is described in Chapter 1 of *Lake Fishing With A Fly*, by Ron Cordes and Randall Kaufmann. You will need to enlarge the bathymetric maps to use them for this purpose.

Because of the book's purpose, I have chosen to omit sections about lake fishing strategies and equipment. This information is covered in detail by several different publications and does not need to be repeated. *Lake Fishing with a Fly*, by Ron Cordes and Randall Kaufmann, and *Strategies for Stillwater*, by Dave Hughes, are two of many excellent resources containing a wealth of information for the lake fly fisher. Thorough study and use of their information will not only increase the angler's skill and knowledge, but also give a greater understanding and appreciation of the aquatic environment, and the many complex, interrelated factors at work under the surface of a lake.

Since regulations have a habit of changing, specifics are not included. Most of the lakes listed are managed, more or less, as quality fisheries and have corresponding regulations. It is the responsibility of each angler to know and follow the regulations for the waters being fished. I will indicate, such as [SPECIAL REGULATIONS], at the beginning of each lake description whether the lake, at the time of this writing, has any special regulations. A current copy of the Washington State Fishing Regulations Pamphlet must be reviewed for specifics.

This brings to mind a conversation I had one day with a fellow angler. He was fishing a damsel nymph imitation along the reeds at Chopaka Lake in the early spring, and couldn't keep the fish off—one good fish after another. At the camp that evening, another angler approached him and asked what he was using. He told him that a damsel nymph fished along the reeds was the hot ticket, and even gave him olive marabou and hooks to tie some imitations. The next day with his newly-tied flies, this other angler began to catch fish. Each one was taken out of the water and dumped into the boat. Chopaka is a fly-fishing-only lake with a one-fish limit, and this angler clearly had killed several fish. When approached about it he said something like, My mom and dad wanted some fish to eat. An angler like this not only hurts himself and others, but also the future of the sport.

Access to the lakes listed in this book is very good. The majority of them can be driven to and are relatively easy to find, several require a walk-in, and some can be tough to find. Four-wheel-drive and high clearance vehicles are seldom needed, although helpful in certain situations. Serious theft of valuable property has occurred at several locations listed in this book, and it is wise to pay special attention to this matter. Parking areas for popular fishing spots are experiencing the same growing theft problem as the parking areas for many of today's popular hiking trails. Please do not make it profitable for those who practice this crime; unattended vehicles loaded with fishing gear are prime targets. Locks will not help a great deal as windows can easily be smashed. Also, theft pros can pick your locks almost as fast as you can open them with a key. Leave nothing of value in open view, or better yet, do not leave anything of value in the vehicle period. Do whatever is necessary to discourage theft.

The best times to fish the lakes listed in this book are generally from April through the first half of June, and the last half of September through November (if the season is open). This is due to water temperature and fish activity, and can vary a bit from year to year depending on the weather. Several of the lakes listed at higher elevations fish well through summer, and are good bets when the others are just too warm.

The most comprehensive overall map for the state is the *Washington Atlas and Gazetteer*, published by the DeLorme Mapping Company. It is by far one of the most-used items I own, offering topographic maps of the entire state, geographic features, highways and backroads, outdoor recreation, township and range system, etc. It is a "must-have" item for sportsmen. Because of its value to the angler as a compact, statewide reference and guide resource, I have referred to it at the beginning of each lake listing. The United States Geological Survey topographic maps, another excellent resource, are indispensable for detailed reference, locating, exploring, and route-finding situations. I also refer to these maps at the beginning of each lake listing. Additional maps that have been useful for specific situations include Green Trails maps and Forest Service maps. Collecting, organizing, and studying maps is an active part of successful lake angling. Contact tackle shops, fly clubs, resorts and campgrounds, Forest Service offices, and Fisheries offices—gather as much information as possible.

Giving fish sizes for a lake, despite first-hand experience and reliable local knowledge, can be a risky thing when accuracy is the goal. Lakes are a living entity, constantly changing in response to a great variety of natural and unnatural factors. Because of this, fishing conditions, fish sizes, fish populations, and even fish species may vary for any number of reasons. Saying that a lake holds fish to 20-plus inches may be true for some years and not others. This should be looked at more as a measure of a lake's potential than a statement of present-day fact. Aside from a natural or man-made disaster, a lake that produces large, healthy fish should continue to do so for many years.

As always, the fly angler who consistently takes the most and best trout understands how the underwater world of a lake functions, and has learned to determine the following:

1. The location of fish and their food sources.
2. The most available and preferable food sources.
3. How to best present an effective imitation of these food sources by experimenting with depth fished, speed of retrieve, and fly pattern, changing one or more of these variables until a successful combination is found.

The Lakes: An Overview
What Are the Regions?

Region 1: Asotin, Columbia, Ferry, Garfield, Lincoln, Pend Oreille, Spokane, Stevens, Walla Walla, and Whitman counties. Region 1 offers outstanding trout fishing and has the second-highest number of productive trout lakes in the state. Geographic features include the Selkirk, Huckleberry, and Kettle River ranges of the Rocky Mountains; the Waterville Plateau, Channeled Scablands, Palouse Hills, and Snake River Valley of the

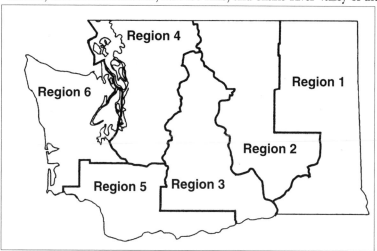

Columbia Basin; and the Blue Mountains, a fragmented section of the Rocky Mountains.

Region 2: Adams, Douglas, Franklin, Grant, and Okanogan counties.

Region 2 is Washington's trout-fishing mecca, containing the highest number of productive trout lakes in the state. Like Region 1, its geographic features are quite diverse—the rugged Okanogan Mountains and pastoral Okanogan Highlands, eastern parts of the incredible North Cascades, the fertile Okanogan and Columbia River valleys, and sections of the Columbia Basin—Saddle Mountains, Quincy Basin, Waterville Plateau, Channeled Scablands and Coulees.

Region 3: Benton, Chelan, Kittitas, and Yakima counties. Productive trout lakes can be hard to find in Region 3. Outside of the high mountain areas, natural lakes in Region 3 can almost be counted on the fingers of one hand. Most of its natural lakes lie in glacier-carved depressions of the Cascade Range. Geographic features include eastern sections of the magnificent central and southern Cascade Range, and sections of the Columbia Basin—Boylston and Saddle Mountains, Umtanum, Ahtanum, Toppenish, and Yakima Ridges, Rattlesnake and Horse Heaven Hills, Kittitas Valley, Yakima Valley, and Pasco Valley.

Region 4: Island, King, Pierce, San Juan, Skagit, Snohomish, and Whatcom counties. Region 4 contains relatively few productive trout lakes. A large number of its lakes are nestled in the glacier-formed depressions of the Cascade Range; the remainder, and most productive, are distributed throughout the Puget Sound Lowlands. Its contrasting geographic features comprise a large portion of the spectacular and awe-inspiring north, central, and south central Cascades, and the picturesque islands, harbors, and valleys of the Puget Sound Lowlands.

Region 5: Clark, Cowlitz, Klickitat, Lewis, Skamania, and Wahkiakum counties. Region 5, similar to Region 3, has a small number of natural lakes outside of the high mountain areas. Nearly all of its lakes lie in depressions of glacial origin in the southern Cascade Range. Geographic features include mighty peaks of the Southern Cascades, Willapa Hills, and the Chehalis, Cowlitz, and Columbia River valleys of the lowlands.

Region 6: Clallam, Grays Harbor, Jefferson, Kitsap, Mason, Pacific, and Thurston counties. Region 6 has few productive trout lakes, however, it is blessed with stunning, contrasting, and unique geographic features—the jagged, ice-capped Olympic Mountain Range which contains many of the region's lakes, Olympic Peninsula rain forests (temperate rain forests with the world's largest of several different coniferous tree species), Willapa Hills, islands and harbors of the Puget Sound Lowlands, Strait of Juan de Fuca, and the rugged Pacific Ocean coastline.

By now I am sure you have asked, "why do regions 1 and 2 have so many productive lakes, while Regions 3-6 offer so few in comparison? Why is there such a difference between the lakes of eastern and western Washington? What makes a lake biologically productive or eutrophic (literally well nourished)? What makes a lake biologically unproductive or oligotrophic (literally little nourished)?" These are worthy questions, deserving an answer.

What Makes a Lake Productive?

Fertile lakes are known for having features that include "hard," nutrient-rich, alkaline water and an average water visibility under 15 feet; gradual bottom slopes with an abundance of organic sediment; extensive, sunstruck, littoral zones; and a productive food chain of abundant aquatic flora and fauna.

Infertile lakes are characterized by features that include "soft," nutrient-poor, acidic water and an average water visibility over 20 feet; steep bottom slopes that are relatively free of organic sediment; small, narrow littoral zones out of proportion to their depths; and small amounts of aquatic flora and fauna. These lakes often have very clear, pure, and beautiful water. Their very beauty, however, indicates an inability to sustain great quantities of aquatic life.

The biological characteristics of a lake are composed of interdependent and interactive physical, chemical, and climatic factors. Plants and animals in a lake depend upon these factors for their very existence. On the other hand, the activities of both plants and animals can produce definite changes in the physical and chemical properties of the lake. Because of this interdependency, lakes are best studied and observed as ecosystems.

Physical and Chemical Factors—Light is of fundamental importance in the ecology of a lake and its productivity. Sunlight is the single most important source of energy, warming the lake and controlling much of its very metabolism. The absorption of sunlight by photosynthetic plants and their resulting growth (provided there are ample nutrients and sediments for growth and attachment) is the basis for the rest of the aquatic food chain.

Upon this foundation, several essential factors often dictate the biological productivity of a lake, within the climatic constraints of its location: the shape of a lake's basin and surrounding topography, chemical structure of rocks and soil in the drainage basin, and size of the drainage area.

A lake basin with a gradual bottom slope has extensive littoral (shallow) zones allowing both the penetration of life-giving light over a large region of the lake bottom and the accumulation of nutrient-rich, organic sediments. (The bottom slope of a lake's basin is often determined by the shape of the surrounding topography.) In general, the littoral zone of a lake extends downward from the shore to either the limit of rooted aquatic plants or the limit of light penetration. Productive littoral (pronounced the same as literal) zones are normally 15 feet and less in depth, although they can reach depths of up to 25 feet depending on water transparency. Also, lake shorelines with an irregular shape, broken by points, coves, and islands, offer a variety of littoral structure and provide protection for submersed aquatic vegetation from the destructive effects of wave action. The above factors play an essential part in creating a suitable environment for the submersed vegetation that provides food, energy, and habitat for a multitude of aquatic critters. Thick bottom sediments of decayed organic matter also accumulate from heavy growths of submersed aquatic vegetation. These bottom sediments are rich in vital nutrients. As water movement stirs up the sediments, nutrients are cycled through the food chain and utilized.

The quantity of dissolved nutrients in the water is essential to the vitality of the entire food chain, from the smallest microscopic organisms to the largest weed beds and fish. The presence or absence of these nutrients is governed to a large degree by the chemical and structural make-up of the rocks and soil in the drainage area. Vital minerals and nutrients, aside from atmospheric exchange, are delivered to a lake by way of either run-off water or groundwater seepage (springs). As water flows over and through the different types of soil and rock, it dissolves essential chemical compounds and minerals, transporting them to the lake. Because of this action, the mineral content and structure of the surrounding land is vital. Dense, non-porous, and insoluble soils and rocks surrender few nutrients. Whereas, porous, soluble, and exposed types of soil and rock yield more nutrients. Both the method and rate nutrient-bearing water is introduced into a lake is determined by the shape of surrounding topography and size of the drainage area. A large drainage area relative to a lake's volume usually results in a high flushing rate. This can really limit nutrient concentration levels. Nutrients that are known to contribute to the fertility of a lake include carbon, phosphorous, nitrogen, calcium, magnesium, potassium, manganese, sulfur, and iron.

Water clarity or visibility is an important indicator of biological productivity. It is a gross measure of phytoplankton (microscopic aquatic plants, or algae) concentrations in the water. Lakes with dense concentrations of plankton and limited transparency are often excellent producers of fish. Plankton and algae are dependent upon essential nutrients available in the water. A lake with high nutrient levels will therefore have abundant quantities of plankton, resulting in limited water transparency. Exceptions to this, as always, do occur—the presence of inorganic turbidity (suspended silt or clay) or dissolved organic matter in the water can give a false indication of high productivity.

Water clarity also varies throughout the year in response to changing plankton densities. For example, a lake might have 8 feet of visibility in April, 16 feet in May, 4 feet in August, and 7 feet in September. A common occurrence in productive lakes that directly affects water visibility is known as an algal bloom. A bloom occurs when water conditions such as chemical makeup and temperature are suitable for prolific growth, which results in a high density of planktonic algae in the water. This condition really limits visibility and gives the water a distinct pea green color. Upon decomposition, algae may also form objectionable scum and odors. An algal bloom can certainly produce difficult fishing conditions; however, it indicates that the lake is well nourished and has potential for growing large fish.

Climatic Factors—One of the primary differences between western and eastern Washington is the climate. Western Washington is characterized by high annual precipitation and moist air; mild, annual temperatures; and overcast skies, resulting in decreased solar radiation. Eastern Washington is known for low annual precipitation and dry air, more extreme temperatures with long, warm summers and relatively short, cold winters, and clear skies with increased solar radiation.

Large amounts of rain (which itself is very "soft" and acidic) can dilute nutrient concentration levels in a lake, and create a high flushing rate where many of the nutrients gathered from the surrounding rocks and soil are washed away. On the other hand, low levels of rainfall, sun and heat, dry air, and wind combine to create high rates of evaporation. As lake water is dispersed by evaporation, essential nutrients are left behind in much greater levels of concentration. Seasonal climatic changes alter the rate of evaporation, rate of photosynthesis, and the amount of run-off and seepage. These changes have a direct influence on the concentration levels of dissolved nutrients in a lake.

How Can You Help?

Due to the value of Washington's most productive lakes, it is essential that each angler take a personal interest in maintaining and improving the quality of fishing in these special places—catch and release plays a vital part in this undertaking. We cannot expect to catch large, healthy trout on a consistent basis unless we leave fish in the water and give nature a chance to grow them—it takes time.

A productive lake's ability to produce numerous large trout is severely hindered if each angler kills even one fish every time he/she fishes it. There is nothing wrong with killing and eating fish; however, this should be confined mostly to the lakes managed for harvest purposes. Many of the state's productive lakes have high algal densities and good amounts of weed growth and muck. This environment usually creates bad-tasting and poor-eating fish. Because of this, it is best to release fish, even though regulations may allow for fish harvest. Anglers who consistently harvest fish grown by the most productive lakes in the state are only hindering quality sport fishing, as some of these lakes are capable of offering world-class fishing for good numbers of large fish if only given the opportunity. Just imagine this kind of fishing without having to travel thousands of miles or spend lots of money! If you do not already practice catch and release, give it a shot. Many anglers find it to be both rewarding and fulfilling—I know you will also.

Please be sure and pinch down the barbs on every hook you own. Not only is it illegal to fish with barbed hooks at most of the lakes in this book, but also barbed hooks tear up the mouth of a fish when removed and make the entire process difficult both for you and the fish. You also will hook more fish with barbless hooks as there is no barb to impede penetration. And, by all means, leave fish in the water when removing the hook. I see so many anglers remove fish from the water into a boat, on a float tube apron, or onto the shore. The fish is thrashing around and the angler is trying to grab it to remove the hook and return the fish to the water. There is no reason to do this! The process of handling and squeezing fish, not to mention suffocation while out of the water, greatly reduces the chance of survival after being released into the water. Please make every effort to release fish in a responsible manner.

As angler pressure increases, it not only becomes important to regard the past few paragraphs, but also the fact that wear and tear on the lakes will increase. Each angler should carry a gallon-sized ziplock bag or garbage sack to pick up fishing litter (leader materials, etc.) and other typical litter from the lake shore or shallow lake bottom. Lakes are a valuable resource and ours to maintain. Let's not allow them to be spoiled by a few uncaring people.

Finally, it is vitally important that we voice our ideas, concerns, and appreciations to the Director of Fish and Wildlife regarding management issues. One present issue of concern for anglers and other sportsmen has to do with the use of rotenone being threatened. Rotenone is a substance derived from the root of various tropical plants, and is used to remove unwanted fish species from lakes that have too much competition for the available insect life. It causes fish to suffocate by inhibiting oxygen absorption. Rotenone is used widely by fish biologists not only in trout lakes that are contaminated with non-trout species, but also in warm water fisheries to improve the population balance and size distribution of certain warm water species. In addition to both trout and warm water fisheries, rotenone is used to improve waterfowl populations. Some of the state's best trout fisheries (Nunnally lakes chain, etc.), not to mention warm water fisheries and waterfowl lakes, will eventually be lost to unwanted fish-species contamination if the use of rotenone is discontinued. (Its use is presently being threatened by people who do not fully understand the issue.) This is occuring due in part to a lack of angler involvement in management issues. The lakes are a valuable resource to sportsmen and ours to maintain.

What About the High Mountain Lakes?

Rich hues of alpenglow, progressing from red, purple, and pink to orange and yellow, painted the clouds and bathed the rugged, alpine peaks with warm color, creating a magical scene, enchanting in its pristine beauty. Still cloaked in pre-dawn shadows, the glassy smooth surface of the lake mirrored this awe-inspiring scene, reflecting it for all to see. This reflection, however, was eventually broken by the swirls of feeding trout in the shallows, signaling the arrival of choice fishing time.

I made my way to the edge of the lake and eased into casting position. My fly landed lightly on the water's surface and was sipped in without hesitation by a trout. This began a morning of spectacular fishing with solitude, fast action, and beautiful, healthy fish—all in a magnificent, alpine setting. Who could ask for more?

Washington's nearly 3,000 high mountain lakes, formed primarily by local glacial action, are located in the Cascade Range (Regions 2-5), Olympic Range (Region 6), and Rocky Mountains (Region 1). Without a doubt, these mountain ranges offer some of the most awesome and spectacular scenery in the world. The high lakes are surrounded by 3 national parks, 1 national volcanic monument, and 6 national forests: North Cascades, Mount Rainier, and Olympic national parks, Mount Saint Helens National Volcanic Monument, and Mt. Baker/Snoqualmie, Wenatchee, Gifford Pinchot, Okanogan, Colville, and Olympic national forests. The lakes are also surrounded by numerous Wilderness Areas, including the Alpine

Lakes and Indian Heaven wildernesses.

Because of their superior management, productivity, and accessibility, the state's lowland lakes constitute nearly all the listings in this book. It would not be practical for the purposes of this book to list the high mountain lakes; an entire hiking and high lake guide book would be necessary to cover this subject properly. Many of the high lakes are biologically unproductive, known for having slow-growing fish, most of which are small. In addition, numerous high lakes have fish populations that are too high for the already limited available feed, further magnifying the problem. This does not mean that high mountain lakes cannot offer quality fishing—quite the contrary. A number of high lakes offer good action for fat, healthy fish. Fish can live to extended ages in many high lakes because of the colder temperatures and cleaner habitat. (Unlike many of the warmer lowland lakes, the high lakes are normally free of disease, parasites, and predation from fish-eating birds.) As a result, they can achieve impressive sizes where decent amounts of feed and a proper fish population/feed balance exist. (Small fish populations are normally required by these lakes to grow big fish.)

There is a special group of anglers who know of exceptions to the problem of high mountain lakes with small, stunted fish. These anglers are avid hikers who spend countless days throughout the year traversing the mountains from one lake to the next—planting fish, making observations, gathering data, and fishing. They know of those special lakes with nice, fat fish and incredible scenery—their secrets are hard won. If you come upon one of these jewels and fish it, realize its value and the fragile aquatic balance on which it hangs. Fish populations in these lakes are small, making either catch and release or very low fish harvest essential to the preservation of their quality angling.

Finally, whether you catch small, stunted fish or healthy 7-pound trout, Washington's high mountain lakes offer unforgettable scenery and experiences, along with a lifetime worth of hiking, fishing, and exploring opportunities—they are definitely worth the effort.

The Lakes: A Guide

The following lake descriptions represent many of Washington's finest trout lakes for fly fishing. Several are my personal favorites. Much pleasure is also to be had in exploring and discovering for ourselves those special lakes not listed in any book. Go out with your favorite flies and give the lakes your best shot! Study them, fish them, question and observe other anglers on the water, make note of important things you see and hear—be observant. Prepare for the pleasure they will bring. You won't be disappointed!

Browns Lake.

Region 1

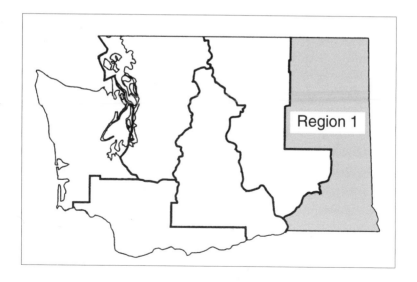

Region 1

Big Four Lake

	106	107	108	109	110	111	112	113	114	115	116	117	118	119
90	91	92	93	94	95	96	97	98	99	100	101	102	103	104	105
74	75	76	77	78	79	80	81	82	83	84	85	86	87	88	89
58	59	60	61	62	63	64	65	66	67	68	69	70	71	72	73
	58	44	45	46	47	48	49	50	51	52	53	54	55	56	57
	58	30	31	32	33	34	35	36	37	38	39	40	41	42	43
				22	23	24	25	26	27	28	29				

Washington Atlas &
Gazetteer Mapping
Grid

Big Four Lake is located in the Tucannon River Canyon on the northern edge of the Blue Mountains in the southeast corner of Washington. It is about 2 miles northeast of the Camp Wooten State Park and Environmental Learning Center, and 4 miles north of the Wenaha/Tucannon Wilderness boundary. The lake lies about 100 yards east of the Tucannon River within Columbia County (T9N R41E S15), 15 miles south of Pomeroy. (See *Washington Atlas and Gazetteer* pg. 42, B-3 and U.S.G.S. Hopkins Ridge.) [SPECIAL REGULATIONS]

Big Four Lake lies at an elevation of 2,535 feet and covers 4.7 surface acres. It has a beautiful setting, hemmed in on the east and west by forested ridges of the Blue Mountains. The Blue Mountains have abundant wildlife and the angler has an excellent chance of seeing white-tailed deer, elk, bear, birds of prey, etc. The ridge rising directly above the

Pomeroy

The town of Pomeroy (15 miles north of Bi[...] rounded by wheat fields; grain elevators [...] ments—they are its life blood, its very [...] early beginnings of this town find th[...] method of subsistence.

Joseph Pomeroy and his wif[...] opened a stage station here [...] Lewiston/Walla Walla stag[...] station twice a day, on[...] only one other family [...] waters in the Blue[...] stage line pers[...] gers. Mrs. P[...]

"I ha[...] table [...] acc[...]

Four Lake) is sur-
and farming imple-
existence. However, the
eir roots in a contrasting

e, with their two young children,
on Pataha Creek in 1864 along the
route. The stage came through their
eastbound and one westbound. In 1864
lived along Pataha Creek, which has its head-
Mountains at Stentz Spring. The owner of the
aded Mrs. Pomeroy to cook meals for the passen-
meroy later reminisced:

told Mr. King that I had nothing to work with, no stove,
r dishes; nothing to cook and I did not see how I could
mmodate him . . .

"Mr. King told me to make a list of what I needed for my house so I could feed his passengers, and, finally, after much urging, I did so. He took my list to Walla Walla, had the bill filled, put on a freight team the next day and brought me a big, nice cookstove with all the things belonging to it; lots of dishes and linen, and said I could pay him when I made the money and could spare it.

"The very next day I gave a dinner to ten passengers, and, oh, didn't they brag on that dinner. I never will forget all the nice things they said."

The stage stop grew quickly into a town with the growth and shipment of wheat as its foundation. When Garfield County was created in 1881, a heated competition for the county seat arose between Pomeroy and a neighboring town a few miles east called Pataha. Pomeroy was finally awarded the distinction of Garfield County seat. During this time the very existence of a community could be assured by becoming designated the county seat. As testimony to this, Pomeroy is now a stable, growing town, whereas Pataha hardly exists.

damselflies, and snails.

Big Four is an artificial lake, created by the Department of Game around 1955 from a gravel pit that was used in building the Tucannon Road. In order to get water to the pit, an inlet stream channel was made from Tucannon River to the southeast corner of the lake. The beginning of the inlet channel near the river has a revolving screen to keep river fish from entering the lake. An outlet was also built that drains from the southwest corner of the lake a short distance to the Tucannon River. Submersed aquatic vegetation is sparse. All of the few lakes that exist in Columbia County are artificial since the soil type and ground water conditions are not conducive to the formation of natural lakes.

Due to the shoreline configuration and small size of Big Four Lake, fishing from any floating device is prohibited. This presents the sometimes difficult challenge of keeping one's fly in the water and out of the surrounding trees and brush. The alert fly fisher not only has a good chance of preventing personal fly loss to the ravenous vegetation, but also of finding those flies which have gleefully escaped from their unfortunate owners by hiding in trees, grass, brush, and whatever else they can find. As you can well imagine, it does not take very many fly fishers to crowd the available fishing space.

To reach Big Four Lake from Highway 12, 4 miles west of Pomeroy, turn south at the 388-mile marker onto Marengo Road which immediately crosses over Pataha Creek. (Maps show the road as Highway 126.) Marengo Road climbs to the top of the nearby hills and eventually becomes gravel, descending by way of sharp curves and switchbacks to Marengo and the Tucannon River Canyon. After 4.1 miles the road comes to Marengo and the Tucannon River Road intersection. Turn left onto the Tucannon Road and travel 15.7 miles to the Big Four Lake parking area turnoff, which is a small, steep, unmarked, dirt driveway on the left side of the Tucannon Road. From the parking area, wade across the Tucannon River (a steel cable stretches across the small river to assist those who need help in crossing) and walk to the lake.

Medical Lake

	106	107	108	109	110	111	112	113	114	115	116	117	118	119
90	91	92	93	94	95	96	97	98	99	100	101	102	103	104	105
74	75	76	77	78	79	80	81	82	83	84	85	86	87	88	89
58	59	60	61	62	63	64	65	66	67	68	69	70	71	72	73
	58	44	45	46	47	48	49	50	51	52	53	54	55	56	57
	58	30	31	32	33	34	35	36	37	38	39	40	41	42	43
			22	23	24	25	26	27	28	29				

Washington Atlas &
Gazetteer Mapping
Grid

Medical Lake is located in Spokane County (T24N R41E
S18,19), 12 miles southwest of Spokane and adjacent to
the town of Medical Lake. (See *Washington Atlas and Gazetteer* pg.
88, D-3 and U.S.G.S. Medical Lake.) [SPECIAL REGULATIONS]

Medical Lake covers 160 surface acres at an altitude of 2,394
feet. Maximum depth is 60 feet with a mean depth of 32 feet. It is a
"kolk" lake (kolk is German for deep pool, scour, hole eroded by
rushing water), situated in eastern Washington's channeled scablands.
The Medical Lake Waterfront Park is located at the southwest corner
of the lake, and the town of Medical Lake lies on the rim above the
lake's east side. The setting is both urban and park-like, yet somewhat
rugged, as rocky, partially timbered land fringes the southeast and
west shorelines.

Biologically speaking, Medical Lake is quite productive. It has a
very high dissolved-mineral concentration and algal density—one of
the highest in the state. A pea soup-colored algal bloom can be
observed during the summer with very limited water visibility. Medical
Lake is sustained entirely by groundwater seepage, which is typical of

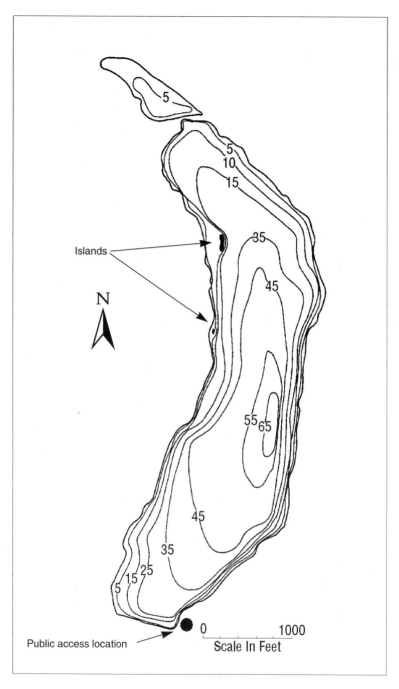

Islands

N

55 65

Public access location

0   1000
Scale In Feet

Morning at Medical Lake.

many lakes in the channeled scablands. The littoral bottom is steep and rocky with relatively light growths of submersed aquatic vegetation. The heaviest growth is confined to the shallow, gradually-sloping areas of the lake (primarily the north and south ends). Reed growth is scattered and covers about 1/5 of the shoreline.

The name Medical Lake originated from the lake's ability to heal physical ailments. In the early 1900s one of the state's first popular resorts was located here. Special healing soaps, tablets, and remedies were made; pits were even dug in town and filled with healing sediments. Today the town library has advertisements displayed from this

Medical Lake.

era. One such advertisement reads: "We can cure you of rheumatism, skin diseases, stomach and kidney trouble by the use of Medical Lake Mud and Water Baths—each mud bath consists of steam bath, hot fresh mud bath, shower, blanket pack and massage."

Medical Lake is stocked with brown trout that average 12-16 inches. Larger fish to 20 or more inches are also present in the lake. Brown trout, especially the older and wiser ones, are habitual night feeders and commonly prey upon small fish. Greatest fishing success will usually be during the low-light hours of the day. Insect life in the lake is relatively abundant with many of the usual critters. Forage fish and leeches are also available. Some bass and panfish are present in the lake and compete with trout for available feed.

To reach Medical Lake from Interstate 90, take the Highway 902 exit for Medical Lake and Cheney. Drive west on 902 (Salnave Road) toward Lakeland Village for 5.5 miles (.15 mile past the left turn for Medical Lake Waterfront Park) to the left turn for public boat launch access. Drive .15 mile on a narrow gravel road to the lake.

Amber Lake

106	107	108	109	110	111	112	113	114	115	116	117	118	119
90 91 92 93 94 95	96	97	98	99	100	101	102	103	104	105			
74 75 76 77 78 79	80	81	82	83	84	85	86	87	88	89			
58 59 60 61 62 63	64	65	66	67	68	69	70	71	72	73			
5? 44 45 46 47	48	49	50	51	52	53	54	55	56	57			
58 30 31 32 33 34	35	36	37	38	39	40	41	42	43				
22 23 24 25 26	27	28	29										

Washington Atlas & Gazetteer Mapping Grid

Amber Lake is located in Spokane County (T22N R40E S36 and T21N R40E S1,2), 10 miles southwest of Cheney. (See *Washington Atlas and Gazetteer* pg. 72, B-3 and U.S.G.S. Amber.) [SPECIAL REGULATIONS]

Amber Lake, formerly called Calvert Lake, lies at an altitude of 2,160 feet and covers 120 surface acres at high water. Maximum depth is 40 feet with a mean depth of 17 feet. Like Medical Lake, Amber Lake is a kolk lake situated in the channeled scablands of eastern Washington. (See section in Region 2 after Dry Falls Lake on Grand Coulee and Dry Falls.) The lake is part of an agricultural area and lies in a gully between moderate basalt cliffs. Rolling hills, wheat fields, pasture and grazing land, and scattered areas of pine trees provide a pastoral, dry land backdrop. Shoreline development is very limited with a few homes along the lake's east half.

Amber Lake is sustained by groundwater seepage, and during spring of wetter years a very small stream drains from the far southwest end of the lake. The water level normally varies a few feet each year and more in dry years. Much of the littoral zone is

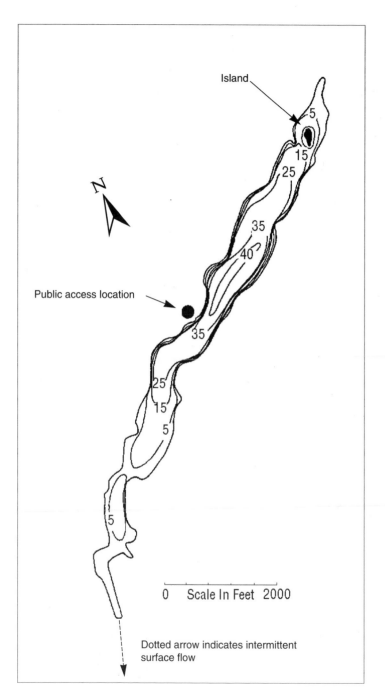

Island

N

Public access location

0   Scale In Feet   2000

Dotted arrow indicates intermittent
surface flow

Amber Lake.

very steep and rocky with gradual sloping areas at the northeast and southwest ends. These shallow, gradual sloping areas support a heavy growth of submersed aquatic vegetation. Aquatic food sources are abundant including mayflies, caddisflies, midges, damselflies, dragonflies, snails, scuds, and leeches.

Rainbow and cutthroat trout in Amber Lake are active and in excellent condition. Most fish will be 12-18 inches with larger fish to 20-plus inches. Amber Lake is near the city of Spokane and is popular with many fly anglers. The heaviest fishing pressure is at the southwest half of the lake. This is mostly due to the location of the public access area, not the lack of good fishing at the lake's northeast half.

To reach Amber Lake from Interstate 90, take the Highway 904 exit toward Tyler and Cheney. Head east for .25 mile and you will come to a sign for "B" street in Tyler. Turn south on "B" street and continue along as it crosses the railroad tracks and becomes Pine Spring Road. Follow Pine Spring Road (bearing left at the 8.4 mile point and T-intersection) until the 11 mile point from Tyler to the signed public fishing access turnoff. Turn right at the sign and drive for 1/2 mile to the public access for Amber Lake. The boat ramp there has been closed for a couple of years due to low water levels.

Browns Lake

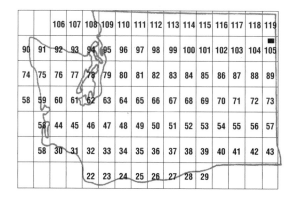

Washington Atlas & Gazetteer Mapping Grid

B rowns Lake is located in Pend Oreille County (T34N R44E S13,24) 9.5 miles northeast of Usk. (See *Washington Atlas and Gazetteer* pg. 105, A-7 and U.S.G.S. Browns Lake.) [SPECIAL REGULATIONS]

Browns Lake covers 84 surface acres and lies at an altitude of 3,411 feet. Maximum depth is 23 feet with a mean depth of 13 feet. These figures are for high water level as Browns Lake commonly has large water-level fluctuations. The lake is situated in a narrow valley between timbered mountain ridges. Browns Lake can be a very enjoyable place to fish since it offers both a beautiful, pristine setting and good fishing. The only thing that can detract from it is the campground during holidays or popular weekends. The Browns Lake campground is the only shoreline development.

The water-level fluctuation at Browns Lake is due to a sinkhole at the west end of the lake. The water drains underground to Browns Creek, which begins about 1/3 mile southwest of Browns

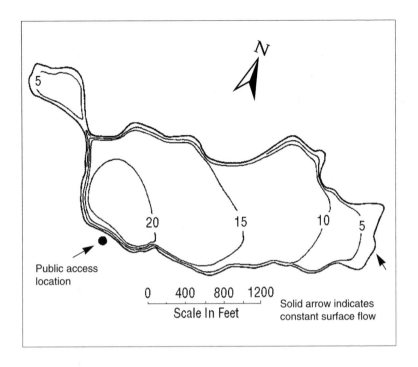

5

20   15   10   5

Public access
location

0   400   800   1200
Scale In Feet

N

Solid arrow indicates
constant surface flow

Lake. A small, partially spring-fed inlet stream flows into the east end of the lake. The nearshore lake bottom is mostly steep and rocky, however, it soon flattens out to form a broad, gradually-sloping bottom area. Grassy meadows at the lake's east end and northwest bay are covered by water at high levels; low water levels expose the meadow areas. The shoreline is covered locally by floating logs and other wood debris. Submersed aquatic vegetation is very sparse and reed growth is almost non-existent. Browns Lake is relatively infertile with high water visibility, low nutrient levels, and a low algal density. The lake is well circulated with high levels of dissolved oxygen throughout the water column.

Browns Lake is stocked with cutthroat trout and despite its relative infertility produces some very beautiful fish. Some limited natural reproduction also takes place in the inlet stream each year. Many cutthroat are rather small, around 8-12 inches. However,

Browns Lake.

some very nice larger fish to 20-plus inches are also available. Many of these large fish have developed a habit of eating little trout.

Access for Browns Lake is from Highway 20 near Usk. Turn from Highway 20 at the sign for Usk and drive east on Kings Lake Road. Continue through Usk and over the Pend Oreille River for 7.4 miles to the sign for Forest Road 5030 and Browns Lake. Turn left on 5030 and drive about 3.5 miles to the Browns Lake campground and parking area above the lake. Boats may be launched by driving down a narrow dirt road to the lake shore. The campground facilities are available on a fee basis.

Manresa Grotto

While you are in the area near Browns Lake, stop and visit Manresa Grotto, located near the Pend Oreille River on the Kalispel Indian Reservation about 6 miles north of Usk and 5 miles southwest of Browns Lake. Manresa Grotto is a

small, above-ground cavern supposedly formed by the waves of a vast, ancient glacial lake. The main section of the cavern (about 25 feet deep and high, and 60 feet long) is a dome-shaped room with rows of flat stones arranged as seats facing a mortared-rock altar.

The cavern was named Grotto of New Manresa in 1844 by Catholic Father Pierre Jean DeSmet. He named it after a famous cave near Barcelona, Spain, in which St. Ignatius (founder of a Roman Catholic order of religious men called the Jesuits) meditated before writing *Spiritual Exercises*, a guidebook to convert the heart and mind to a closer following of Christ.

Pierre Jean DeSmet first came to the Pend Oreille River in the Kalispel Valley near Cusick in 1841, and he wrote these words in November of the same year: "I see a fine location for a mission, where wood will never fail and the river abounds in fish, along the fertile prairie on the west side of the river." Later in 1844, Father Andrew Hoecken, with assistance from DeSmet, established the

Nile Lake

Nile Lake is located in Pend Oreille County (T37N R42E S35), 6 miles southwest of Ione at the south end of Tiger Meadows. (See *Washington Atlas and Gazetteer* pg. 119, C-5 and U.S.G.S. Ione.)

Nile Lake, formerly a private lake called Porters Lake, covers 22 surface acres at an altitude of 3,190 feet. Maximum depth is 28 feet with a mean depth of 17 feet. Nile Lake is less than 1/4 mile east of Highway 20 and offers a very nice, picturesque setting. Timbered mountain ridges create a backdrop to the east and south, and Tiger Meadows, dotted with

St. Ignatius Mission on the present-day Kalispel Reservation. DeSmet wrote, "On returning to the Bay accompanied by Father Hoecken and several chiefs, my first care was to examine the land belonging to this portion of the tribe of Kalispels and select a fit site for the new establishment of St. Ignatius. We found a vast and beautiful prairie three miles in extent, surrounded by cedar and pine, in the neighborhood of the cavern of New Manresa and its quarries..." Both Hoecken and DeSmet, due to the lateness of the season, wintered (1844-45) with the Kalispels of the Bay. DeSmet celebrated a Christmas Mass with these people in the cavern of New Manresa Grotto.

However, the Mission's location was not so ideal as DeSmet first imagined. The land did not produce very well, spring flooding hindered planting, and the menace of starvation caused the Kalispels to grow restless. (It is said that priests and Indians also used Manresa Grotto for shelter during spring flooding of the Pend Oreille River.) After harvest in September of 1854, the majority of the 200 Kalispels of the Bay, under Chief Victor, accompanied the missionaries to the Mission Valley in Montana where they moved the St. Ignatius Mission. Most of the Indians soon returned to the Kalispel Valley. (The present St. Ignatius Mission is located east of St. Ignatius, Montana and is said to be the third most beautiful church in the world. It contains 58 original murals on its walls and ceilings.)

Today the Kalispel Tribe of Indians use Manresa Grotto for annual Mass Services. To get there, drive through Usk and cross over the Pend Oreille River (as if you were heading to Browns Lake). Turn north on Leclerc Creek Road immediately after crossing Pend Oreille River and drive for about 6 miles to the Manresa Grotto sign and parking area on the right side of the road. A short path climbs uphill to the cavern. There are excellent views of the Pend Oreille River and surrounding mountains.

		106	107	108	109	110	111	112	113	114	115	116	117	118	119
90	91	92	93	94	95	96	97	98	99	100	101	102	103	104	105
74	75	76	77	78	79	80	81	82	83	84	85	86	87	88	89
58	59	60	61	62	63	64	65	66	67	68	69	70	71	72	73
	58	44	45	46	47	48	49	50	51	52	53	54	55	56	57
	58	30	31	32	33	34	35	36	37	38	39	40	41	42	43
				22	23	24	25	26	27	28	29				

Washington Atlas & Gazetteer Mapping Grid

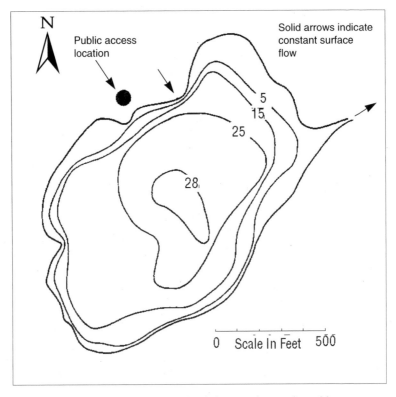

grazing cattle, provides a pastoral backdrop to the north. Public access is at the northwest side of the lake. There is no nearshore development.

Nile Lake, in a sense, is an enlargement of Lost Creek which flows into the north end of the lake and drains to the northeast. The water has a distinct amber hue caused by tannic acid from the decomposition of plant matter. Nile Lake is a moderately productive lake that supports many of the usual aquatic trout foods such as damselflies, dragonflies, leeches, midges, mayflies, caddisflies, and snails. The littoral bottom is covered with a short growth of submersed aquatic vegetation. The shoreline of Nile Lake is entirely covered with reeds, and lily pads cover the lake surface in a narrow margin close to shore.

Nile Lake has been managed for brook trout over the years and has produced some nice fish to 14 or more inches. Most brook trout will be 8-14 inches. The brook trout successfully spawn each year in addition to some supplementary stocking. Efforts were started in the fall of 1993 by the Department of Fisheries to manage Nile Lake for a stocked strain of wild rainbow trout. Some pumpkin seed sunfish exist in the lake and it is hoped that the rainbow trout will eat the sunfish fry and eventually outcompete the sunfish. If this happens, the rainbows should do very well in Nile Lake. Most rainbow trout will be in the 8- to 14-inch range with occasional larger fish available. Since Nile Lake has standard harvest regulations and will receive harvest pressure every year, the average fish size and number of large fish available are smaller than they could be with special harvest regulations. Watch for Nile Lake to improve in the coming years.

Access for Nile Lake is from Highway 20 at the head of the Little Pend Oreille River Valley. From Highway 20 in Colville (at the stoplight intersection where Highway 20 turns east toward Ione and the Little Pend Oreille National Wildlife Refuge), drive east for 31 miles on Highway 20 to the turnoff for Nile Lake on the right side of the highway. The lake can be seen looking east from the highway. Drive downhill on a dirt road for about 1/4 mile to the northwest part of the lake.

Nile Lake.

Rigley Lake

	106	107	108	109	110	111	112	113	114	115	116	117	118	119
90	91	92	93	94	95	96	97	98	99	100	101	102	103	104	105
74	75	76	77	78	79	80	81	82	83	84	85	86	87	88	89
58	59	60	61	62	63	64	65	66	67	68	69	70	71	72	73
	59	44	45	46	47	48	49	50	51	52	53	54	55	56	57
	58	30	31	32	33	34	35	36	37	38	39	40	41	42	43
			22	23	24	25	26	27	28	29					

Washington Atlas & Gazetteer Mapping Grid

Rigley Lake is located in Stevens County (T36N R38E S2), 8 miles northwest of Colville on top of Echo Mountain. (See *Washington Atlas and Gazetteer* pg. 118, C-1 and U.S.G.S. Echo Valley.) [SPECIAL REGULATIONS]

Rigley Lake lies at an altitude of 2,531 feet and covers about 6 surface acres. Maximum depth is 32 feet with a mean depth of about 20 feet. The lake is just a small, round hole that lies in a several-acre marshy area surrounded by pine, fir, larch, and aspen trees. It offers a peaceful, personal setting with good trout fishing. However, it takes very few anglers to crowd the available fishing space and change the mood that the nice setting creates.

Since Rigley Lake is situated on top of Echo Mountain, it has a very limited drainage area. The only above-ground inflow it receives is from a tiny runoff stream that flows into the north end of the lake during early spring. The small amount of inflow the lake receives is primarily from groundwater seepage. An outlet stream drains from the southwest corner of the lake to Pingston Creek; it is also intermittent, flowing during spring. The lake level varies 1-2 feet each year.

Rigley Lake has a very steep bottom slope for its size, and the

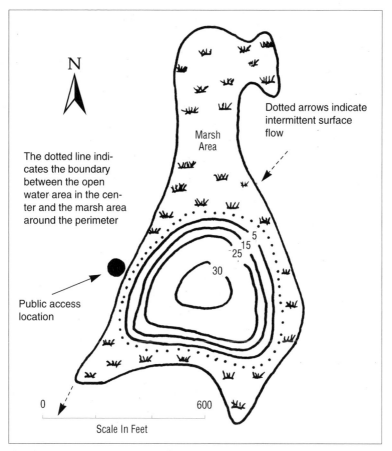

The dotted line indicates the boundary between the open water area in the center and the marsh area around the perimeter

N

Marsh Area

Dotted arrows indicate intermittent surface flow

5
15
25
30

Public access location

0   600

Scale In Feet

depth contours are quite uniform. A narrow shelf up to 3 feet deep encircles the lake and then drops quickly to a depth of 25 feet where the bottom flattens out and gradually descends to a depth of 32 feet at the lake center. The littoral bottom is thick muck and is completely covered with a short, dense growth of submersed aquatic vegetation. A very heavy growth of reeds covers both the entire shoreline and the adjacent marshy area. Aquatic food sources are abundant; leeches are especially prolific.

Rigley Lake has a history of winter-killing every year and it continues that tradition to this day. Rainbow trout are stocked each spring and die each winter. As a result, Rigley Lake relies entirely on its spe-

Submerged weeds and logs at Rigley Lake.

cial regulations to provide good fishing. It would not take very long to fish out the lake; however, it does get poached to some degree (unfortunately like many other lakes). If you go fishing at Rigley Lake (or any other lake), keep an eye out for people trying to skip the regulations. Fish size depends entirely on the spring plant, but usually ranges from 8-14 inches. Large brood fish have also been stocked in past years. Fish grow quickly in Rigley Lake and are active, scrappy fighters. You might want to contact the Region 1 Fisheries office for information about obtaining updated stocking data.

To reach Rigley Lake from Highway 20, 6 miles from the west side of Colville, turn north onto Pingston Creek Road. Drive for 5.5 miles on Pingston Creek Road, and then turn right on a dirt road that begins at the outlet area near the lake's southwest corner. The dirt road goes a short distance to the west side of Rigley Lake. The lake's launching area is used for watering by range cattle and can be a bit messy at times.

Cedar Lake

	106	107	108	109	110	111	112	113	114	115	116	117	118	119
90	91	92	93	94	95	96	97	98	99	100	101	102	103	104	105
74	75	76	77	78	79	80	81	82	83	84	85	86	87	88	89
58	59	60	61	62	63	64	65	66	67	68	69	70	71	72	73
	59	44	45	46	47	48	49	50	51	52	53	54	55	56	57
	58	30	31	32	33	34	35	36	37	38	39	40	41	42	43
			22	23	24	25	26	27	28	29			

Washington Atlas & Gazetteer Mapping Grid

Cedar Lake is located in Stevens County (T40N R41E S26), 30 miles north-east of Colville and 4 miles south of the Canada/U.S. border. (See *Washington Atlas and Gazetteer* pg. 118, A-4 and U.S.G.S. Leadpoint.)

Cedar Lake covers 52 surface acres at an altitude of 2,135 feet.

Cedar Lake.

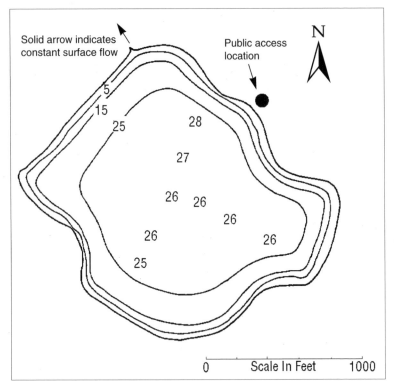

Maximum depth is 28 feet with a mean depth of 24 feet. Cedar Lake is situated in a small valley that runs north and south between timbered ridges. The valley has extensive areas of meadow that surround the lake, with exception of the east side where a few homes and the public access are located. The Deep Lake/Boundary Road also borders part of the lake's east shore. Most of the meadows are used as pasture for horses and cattle. Active mining and logging can also be observed throughout the area.

Cedar Lake is fed by groundwater seepage and drains northerly to Cedar Creek. The water level usually varies a foot or two during the course of a year. The littoral bottom is silt and muck and is completely covered with a short, dense growth of submersed aquatic vegetation. Cedar Lake has a relatively narrow shelf up to 5 feet deep that encircles the lake and then drops quickly into deeper water. The entire shoreline is covered with reeds.

Cedar Lake has an abundance of aquatic food sources such as damselflies, dragonflies, scuds, leeches, midges, mayflies, caddisflies, and snails that nourish its resident rainbow trout. The fish grow quickly and are strong, active, and well-conditioned. Most fish will be 10-16 inches with occasional larger trout to 20-plus inches. Cedar Lake has standard harvest regulations and would produce a higher number of 16- to 20-inch fish with special regulations limiting fish harvest.

To reach Cedar Lake from Highway 20 in Colville (at the stoplight intersection where Highway 20 turns east toward Ione and the Little Pend Oreille National Wildlife Refuge), drive 1.1 miles east and turn from Highway 20 onto Aladdin Road at the sign for Deep Lake Recreation Area. Drive 36.4 miles north (bearing right onto Deep Lake/Boundary Road at the 26.2 mile point and "Y" intersection) to the public access sign at the east side of Cedar Lake.

Rocky Lake

Washington Atlas & Gazetteer Mapping Grid

R ocky Lake is located in Stevens County (T35N R39E 27,34), 3 miles south of Colville. (See *Washington Atlas and Gazetteer* pg. 104, A-2 and U.S.G.S Addy Mountain.) [SPECIAL REGULATIONS]

The dotted lines indi-
cate the location of
the water when
Rocky Lake divides
into 2 small lakes at
very low water levels.

The depths indicated
are approximate for
Rocky Lake at higher
water levels. All
depths outside the
dotted lines are 5 feet
or less.

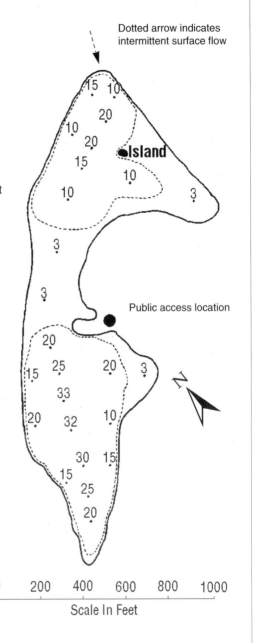

Dotted arrow indicates
intermittent surface flow

Island

Public access location

N

0   200   400   600   800   1000
Scale In Feet

Rocky Lake covers 20 acres at high water level and lies at an altitude of 2,210 feet. Maximum depth is about 33 feet at high water with a mean depth of 10-15 feet. Rocky Lake is situated in a small basin rimmed by rock outcroppings and low hills covered with timber and grassy meadow. A couple of homes sit above the west side of the lake. The setting is unique and attractive and provides a very pleasant backdrop for fishing.

Since Rocky Lake is situated near the top of an elevated region, its drainage area is very limited. Rocky Lake receives inflow primarily from groundwater seepage; drainage takes place underground. An intermittent stream also flows into the northeast end of the lake. A 1/4-acre pond, through which this stream flows, lies 500 feet from the northeast end of the lake. The lake level fluctuates some every year, and at very low water level Rocky Lake divides into 2 lakes—one in the northeast half (about 6 acres) and one in the southwest half (about 8 acres). The narrow area that divides the two lakes is covered by approximately 3 feet of water at high lake level.

Rocky Lake is moderately productive and harbors a good population of some of the usual aquatic insects. The littoral bottom is covered with an excellent growth of weeds, especially the shallower northeast half of the lake and the narrow channel that divides the two

Morning at Rocky Lake.

halves. The shoreline is mostly covered by reed growth; floating logs and other wood debris also cover the shoreline. Rocky Lake is aerated during winter to help prevent winter kill. The aerator has been in use since 1970; the most recent winter kill was during the winter of 1987-88.

Rocky Lake is stocked with rainbow trout each year and is open for one month in the spring under standard regulations (catch and release the remainder of the year). It receives a heavy fish harvest during this time. Most fish will be 8-14 inches with occasional larger fish available. The fish are in good condition and are strong and active fighters. Rocky Lake is not a place where anglers can expect abundant big fish. However, good action for nice fish in an enjoyable setting can be expected.

To reach Rocky Lake from Highway 20 in Colville (at the stoplight intersection where Highway 20 turns east toward Ione and the Little Pend Oreille National Wildlife Refuge), drive 6.1 miles east to Artman Gibson Road and the signs for Rocky Lake and the Little Pend Oreille Wildlife Refuge. Drive south on Artman Gibson Road for 3.3 miles and then turn north on the gravel road at the sign for Rocky Lake. Drive just over 2 miles, staying on the main gravel road, to the public fishing access at the east side of the lake. There is also a camping and picnic area back in the trees above the east side of the lake.

McDowell Lake

		106	107	108	109	110	111	112	113	114	115	116	117	118	119
90	91	92	93	94	95	96	97	98	99	100	101	102	103	104	105
74	75	76	77	78	79	80	81	82	83	84	85	86	87	88	89
58	59	60	61	62	63	64	65	66	67	68	69	70	71	72	73
	58	44	45	46	47	48	49	50	51	52	53	54	55	56	57
	58	30	31	32	33	34	35	36	37	38	39	40	41	42	43
			22	23	24	25	26	27	28	29					

Washington Atlas & Gazetteer Mapping Grid

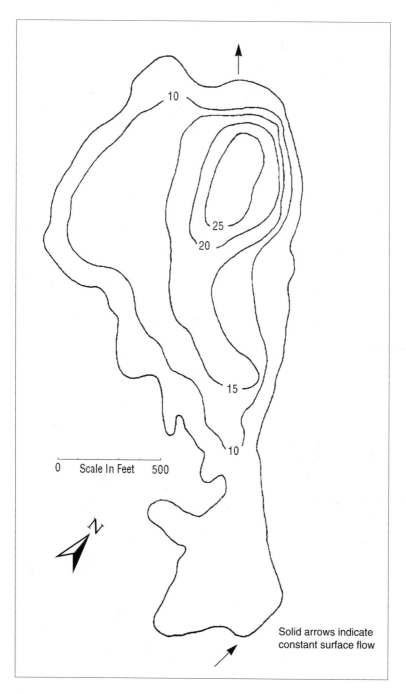

10

25
20

15

10

0   Scale In Feet   500

N

Solid arrows indicate
constant surface flow

McDowell Lake is located in Stevens County (T34N R41E S6,7), 10 miles southeast of Colville on the 41,555-acre Little Pend Oreille National Wildlife Refuge. (See *Washington Atlas and Gazetteer* pg. 104, A-3 and U.S.G.S. Cliff Ridge.) [SPECIAL REGU-LATIONS]

McDowell Lake covers about 33 surface acres at an altitude of 2,325 feet. Maximum depth is about 30 feet with a mean depth of 10-15 feet. McDowell Lake has a tranquil setting, and is surrounded by low, timbered hills. A marsh borders the north end of the lake. The Little Pend Oreille River is about 1/4 mile to the northwest. McDowell Lake has a large waterfowl population, and big game is abundant in the area, especially white-tailed deer. Public access is by way of a path to the lake's north end. There is no nearshore development.

McDowell Lake was originally 2 small lakes of 5.6 and 2.3 acres in a 36-acre marshy area. A dam was first built around 1960 to create a single lake of about 33 surface acres, inundating the 2 small lakes and most of the marshy area. The present earth-fill dam was

McDowell Lake.

constructed by the Department of Game in 1972.

The lake has a high algal density and produces heavy blooms during the summer months. The water has very limited visibility during these times. McDowell Lake is fed by a diversion of the North Fork Bear Creek and drains northerly through the earth-fill dam to the adjacent marsh and Little Pend Oreille River. Submersed aquatic vegetation covers the lake bottom to depths of about 15 feet; it is heavy in some areas and light in others. The shoreline has areas of scattered reed growth, but for the most part, is relatively free of this emersed aquatic vegetation.

McDowell Lake has an excellent population of insect life which should produce fat, healthy trout. The lake does produce a number of fish like this, however, many are not quite as fat as one would expect. This is due to a problem with tench contamination the lake has had since around the late 1970s. (It is said that rainbow trout fishing was extraordinary before the tench contamination.) Tench, a carp-like fish, exist in the lake and compete with trout for available feed. Many pounds of tench have been removed with a trap net, and the lake was rehabilitated several years back; but the tench continued to survive. Brown trout were introduced in 1992 to try and control the tench. Rainbow trout are also stocked and Arctic grayling have been stocked in the past. Most fish will be 12-18 inches with larger trout available. Fishing action, however, can be slow at times, particularly when the lake is blooming with algae and has limited visibility.

To reach McDowell Lake from Highway 20 in Colville (at the stoplight intersection where Highway 20 turns east toward Ione and the Little Pend Oreille National Wildlife Refuge), drive east for 9.5 miles to Kitt/Narcisse Road and the sign for the Little Pend Oreille Wildlife Refuge. Drive south on Kitt/Narcisse Road for 1.5 miles to Narcisse Creek Road. Turn left and drive for 3.5 miles (bear left at the 1.7 mile point and "Y" intersection and then bear to the right immediately after the "Y" intersection) to the small bridge over Little Pend Oreille River. Cross over the bridge and turn off the road immediately to the right; park near the yellow steel bar gate which is a short distance from the bridge. This is where the path to McDowell Lake heads south about 1/3 mile to the north end of the lake. The stream which drains McDowell Lake and flows through the adjacent marsh crosses over this path about halfway to the lake.

Starvation Lake

Washington Atlas & Gazetteer Mapping Grid

Starvation Lake is located in Stevens County (T35N R40E S36), 9 miles east and south of Colville and 2 miles northwest of McDowell Lake. The east end of Starvation Lake is on the 41,555-acre Little Pend Oreille National Wildlife Refuge. (See *Washington Atlas and Gazetteer* pg. 104, A-3 and U.S.G.S. Cliff Ridge.) [SPECIAL REGULATIONS]

Starvation Lake covers 30 surface acres and lies at an altitude of 2,375 feet. Maximum depth is 14 feet with a mean depth of 8 feet. Starvation Lake offers a pleasant, rural setting and is surrounded by grassy hillsides with partially timbered areas of fir, pine, larch, and aspen. Timbered mountain ridges provide a backdrop to the south and west. The east side of the lake lies adjacent to a small marshy area. Nearshore development is limited; there is a cluster of a few homes on the south side of the lake. Big game such as bear, deer, and elk are common in the area and the lake has a large waterfowl population, especially

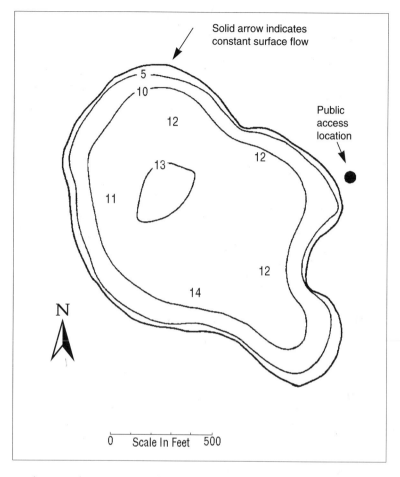

Solid arrow indicates constant surface flow

Public access location

5
10
12
13
12
11
12
14

N

0   Scale In Feet   500

in the marshy area along the east side of the lake. Beaver can be observed during times of low light, and osprey frequently fish at the lake.

The shoreline is completely covered with a heavy growth of reeds, and lily pads cover the lake surface in a narrow margin close to shore. The entire lake bottom is covered with a heavy growth of submersed aquatic vegetation. A small inlet stream flows into the north end of the lake and drainage takes place through underground seepage. Starvation Lake has a history of winter kill and has been aerated during the winter since the mid 1970s to raise dissolved oxygen levels. Despite the aeration, Starvation Lake last killed in the winter of 1992-1993.

Starvation Lake.

Rainbow trout attract anglers to Starvation Lake each year. The fish are pretty and in good condition. Insect life is relatively abundant in the lake, and most fish will be 8-14 inches with occasional larger fish available. Starvation Lake operates under standard regulations for one month in spring (catch and release the remainder of the year) and has a heavy fish harvest during this time. Some of the larger fish that I have caught at Starvation Lake were holding in shallow water next to the lily pads, just waiting for something to pounce on. Dry fly imitations work well in Starvation Lake, especially along the lily pads.

To reach Starvation Lake from Highway 20 in Colville (at the stoplight intersection where Highway 20 turns east toward Ione and the Little Pend Oreille National Wildlife Refuge), drive 10.8 miles east to the sign for Starvation Lake. Turn south on the gravel Starvation Lake Road and follow the signs just over 1 mile to the public access area at the northeast side of the lake.

Bayley Lake

Bayley Lake is located in Stevens County (T34N R41E S29), 12.5 miles southeast of Colville and 3 miles south of McDowell Lake

Washington Atlas & Gazetteer Mapping Grid

on the 41,555-acre Little Pend Oreille National Wildlife Refuge. (See *Washington Atlas and Gazetteer* pg. 104, A-3 and U.S.G.S. Cliff Ridge.) [SPECIAL REGULATIONS]

Bayley Lake, formerly called Cliff Lake, lies at an altitude of 2,400 feet and covers about 72 surface acres at high water and about 18 surface acres at low water. Maximum depth at high water is about 25 feet; maximum depth at low water is about 17 feet.

Bayley Lake is named after a man who owned the lake during the 1920s and 1930s and used it to grow brook trout for commercial markets. It is situated in a canyon between Cliff Ridge to the west and McDonald Mountain to the east. An earth-fill dam at the south end of the canyon (the original dam was built by Bayley around 1920) holds the lake in at high water level. The large water level fluctuation that occurs every year is caused by a sinkhole at the south end of the canyon. At low water level in summer and fall Bayley Lake has a wide, shallow shelf that encircles the lake. The lake bottom then gradually drops to a central area of 10-15 feet in depth. During this time the lake is bordered by about 54 acres of a boggy, peaty meadow. Part of this meadow is used by cattle during the summer months for grazing. The meadow area is covered at high water level by about 6-8 feet of water; the extent to which the meadow is covered in spring depends entirely on the amount of snow melt and precipitation. The lake is bordered on the east and west at high water level by steep, timbered slopes.

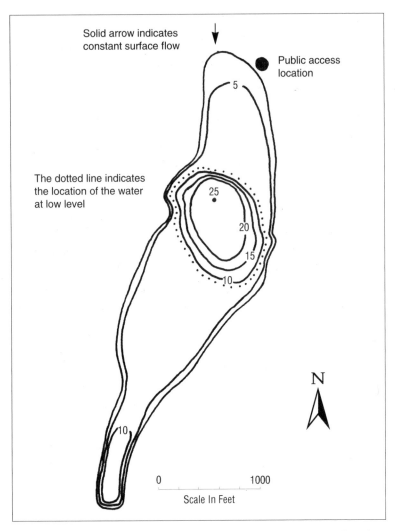

Solid arrow indicates
constant surface flow

Public access
location

5

The dotted line indicates
the location of the water
at low level

25

20

15

10

10

N

0   1000

Scale In Feet

The high water line can be seen on surrounding tree stumps and rocks.

Bayley Lake is fed by a small diversion of the South Fork Bear Creek that flows into the north end of the lake via Potters Pond. The water drains underground from the south end of the lake to Bayley Creek. Submersed aquatic vegetation is relatively sparse, limited to shallow areas that are covered by water throughout the year. Reed growth is virtually non-existent.

Float tube and rods silhouetted against morning reflection at Bayley Lake.

Aquatic food sources are abundant in Bayley Lake and grow healthy rainbow and brook trout. Most fish will be 10-18 inches with some occasional larger trout available. Limited successful spawning occurs to some degree each year, primarily with brook trout. Fishing action is sporadic as the lake is known to be moody—there are times of good action, however, much of the time action is slow.

Access to Bayley Lake requires a number of miles on dirt back-roads. To reach Bayley Lake from Highway 20 in Colville (at the stoplight intersection where Highway 20 turns east toward Ione and the Little Pend Oreille National Wildlife Refuge), drive east for 9.5 miles to Kitt/Narcisse Road and the sign for the Little Pend Oreille Wildlife Refuge. Drive south on Kitt/Narcisse Road for 1.5 miles to Narcisse Creek Road. Turn left and drive for 2.8 miles (bear right at the 1.7 mile point and "Y" intersection) to the road end and "T" intersection at Bear Creek Road. Turn left on Bear Creek Road and drive east for 4.7 miles to a small dirt road that branches off to the right. Turn right and drive for 1.1 miles, past Potters Pond, to the north end of Bayley Lake. During low water levels access is best reached by going along the east side of the canyon for .4 mile on a dirt path to the middle part of the east shore.

Long Lake

	106	107	108	109	110	111	112	113	114	115	116	117	118	119
90	91	92	93	94	95	96	97	98	99	100	101	102	103	104	105
74	75	76	77	78	79	80	81	82	83	84	85	86	87	88	89
58	59	60	61	62	63	64	65	66	67	68	69	70	71	72	73
	58	44	45	46	47	48	49	50	51	52	53	54	55	56	57
	58	30	31	32	33	34	35	36	37	38	39	40	41	42	43
				22	23	24	25	26	27	28	29				

Washington Atlas & Gazetteer Mapping Grid

Long Lake is located in Ferry County (T35N R32E S28,33), 10.5 miles southwest of Republic. (See *Washington Atlas and Gazetteer* pg. 102, A-2 and pg. 116, D-2 and U.S.G.S. Bald Knob.) [SPECIAL REGULATIONS]

Long Lake lies at an altitude of 3,250 feet and covers 24 surface acres. Maximum depth is 58 feet with a mean depth of 18 feet. It is situated in a small, partially timbered canyon on a series of mountain ridges that divide the Aeneas Valley on the west and the San Poil River Valley on the east. The setting is pristine and unspoiled. The only possible distraction is the Long Lake campground during occasional popular holidays or weekends. The campground is located at the far north end of the lake.

Long Lake is fed by groundwater seepage and drains intermittently both to the north toward Fish Lake and Scatter Creek, and to the south toward the West Fork San Poil River. The shoreline is covered with reed growth at the north and south ends of the lake. The east and west shorelines of the lake are covered in scattered areas with floating logs and other wood debris. As the surrounding topography would indicate, Long Lake has a very steep bottom slope and is deep for its size. An excellent

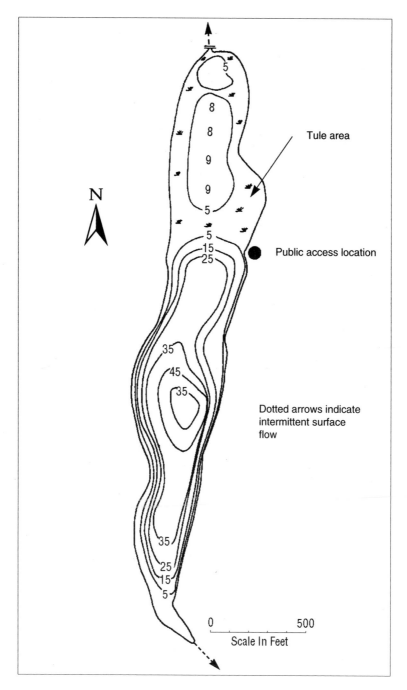

N

Tule area

Public access location

Dotted arrows indicate intermittent surface flow

0   500
Scale In Feet

Long Lake.

growth of submersed aquatic vegetation covers the littoral bottom at the north and south ends of the lake. The heaviest growth of aquatic vegetation in the lake, both emersed (reeds) and submersed, occurs in the shallow area at the north end.

Long Lake harbors a good population of aquatic food sources that include scuds, damselflies, dragonflies, mayflies, caddisflies, snails, and crayfish. The lake is stocked every year with cutthroat trout. Many fish will be in the 8- to 14-inch range with larger fish to 20 inches. Cutthroat trout in Long Lake are beautiful, active fish that can provide a very enjoyable day of fly fishing.

To reach Long Lake from Republic, drive south on Highway 21 toward Keller for 6.9 miles to Scatter Creek Road. Head west on Scatter Creek Road toward Swan Lake for 5.8 miles to the sign for Fish and Long lakes. Drive for .9 miles, past Fish Lake, to the public access and launching area at the north half of Long Lake just south of the shallow, reedy area.

Curlew Lake

Washington Atlas & Gazetteer Mapping Grid

C urlew Lake is located in Ferry County (T38N R33E S29,32 and T37N R33E S5,8,17), 4 miles northeast of Republic and 8.5 miles south of Curlew. (See *Washington Atlas and Gazetteer* pg. 116, C-3 and U.S.G.S. Republic and Karamin.)

Curlew Lake lies at an altitude of 2,333 feet and covers 920 surface acres. Maximum depth is 130 feet with a mean depth of 43 feet. Curlew Lake, called Karanip Lake in 1895, is a natural lake stabilized by a 3-foot dam in 1926. It is situated in a long channel that extends 4.8 miles from south end to north end. There are 4 separate islands, 3 in the south half and 1 in the north half, that total 20 acres in size. Nearshore development is extensive. Curlew Lake has 4 resorts, 2 on the west shore and 2 on the east shore, Curlew Lake State Park and public access is located at the southeast section of the lake, and over 100 homes and cabins are scattered along both sides of the lake— even some of the islands have small cabins on them. The setting, however, is pleasant and attractive with surrounding views of partially timbered mountain ridges.

Curlew Lake is fed by 7 small streams that include Trout, Mires, Barrett, and Herron creeks, and a branch of the San Poil River. There

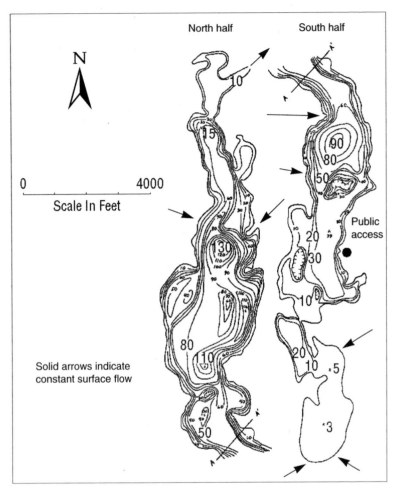

0   4000

Scale In Feet

Public
access

Solid arrows indicate
constant surface flow

is one surface outlet at the far north end of the lake which drains to
Curlew Creek and the Kettle River. The shoreline is quite irregular
with numerous points and coves that provide a variety of littoral structure. The littoral zone is covered in many areas with a heavy growth of
submersed aquatic vegetation that supports an abundant population of
aquatic trout foods such as scuds, damselflies, dragonflies, leeches,
mayflies, snails, and caddisflies. Reeds grow in scattered areas and
cover about 1/3 of the shoreline.

Rainbow trout are stocked in Curlew Lake and grow quickly on its abundant feed. Well-conditioned, active fish averaging 10-16 inches can be expected with larger fish to 20-plus inches available. You might also catch a few brook trout which have been stocked in past years. Some bass have been in Curlew Lake for many years, and so far have not created any problems for the trout. Curlew Lake has standard harvest regulations and receives heavy recreational pressure. An angler looking for a tranquil environment in which to fish will most likely avoid Curlew Lake. However, there are times and places at the lake that provide a very peaceful atmosphere and outstanding fishing.

To reach Curlew Lake from Highway 20 about 3 miles east of Republic, turn north on Highway 21 at the sign for Curlew and drive for 6.1 miles to the signed left turn for Curlew Lake State Park. Drive 1/2 mile from Highway 21 to the state park and boat launch area.

Republic

Four miles southwest of Curlew Lake lies the small town of Republic. Republic is the Ferry County seat with a population of a little over 1,000—one of the smallest county seats in the state. This is due to Ferry County's minimal population, less than stellar economy, and the fact that most land in Ferry County belongs to either the Colville Indian Reservation or the Colville National Forest. Ferry County was named after Elisha P. Ferry, who served from 1889-1893 as Washington state's first Governor.

Typical of many western mining towns, Republic came into existence with a rush. Atypical of many western mining towns, Republic still exists as a stable town. The north half of the Colville Reservation, which encompassed the Republic area, opened to legal mineral exploration on February 21 of 1896. The same day, in the bitter cold, a prospector by the name of John Welty is said to have been the first white man to make a mineral discovery in what would soon become the Eureka Creek Mining District; Welty's first location was the Black Tail claim. On April 18, with a population of 64 men, the Eureka Creek Mining District was formed. (It would later become the Republic Mining District, named after the biggest mine in the area at the time.) Tents and canvas-topped shacks were abundant in the early days of the Eureka camp, soon giving way to frame structures. 1897 brought more miners and those who supplied their needs. Claims were being discovered continually, and those already discovered were developed into mines and producing handsomely.

The present Republic townsite was platted in the early spring of 1898, and within two months nearly 2,000 people came to the town of Republic. Phone service had been connected by May 6 of 1898 and new strikes were reported daily to stock companies in Spokane who gave stock quotations in return. The Republic Pioneer newspaper wrote the following on May 14, 1898: "Here is a little city that is moving right along. L. Hallenbeck, steamboat man said there was 11 acres of freight at the landing and more arriving every day—he said 75 freight wagons could not transport all of it." On June 30 of 1898 the south half of the Colville Reservation opened to legal mineral exploration, creating an even greater need for supplies throughout the county. Republic was booming!

By 1900 a myriad of services had come to Republic: post office (one of the busiest in the state), blacksmith shops, newspapers, general stores, fruit and cigar stores, hotels, barbershops, banks, restaurants, meat markets, livery stables, bakeries, assay offices, tailors, schools, shoemakers, doctors, jewelers, justice court rooms, a Roman Catholic church, and up to 28 saloons! Six dance halls were operating night and day. In 1900 the north half of the Colville Indian Reservation, was opened to homestead and timber claims. This brought a rush of homesteaders, loggers, and sawmills. Before 1900 was history, Republic had quickly become the sixth largest city in the state!

"The mines eventually played out," is the usual western mining town epitaph. This is not entirely true, however, for Republic. Up to the early part of 1900 there were 12,500 mineral locations recorded. The close-to-the-surface type of ore found in the area produced one of the greatest booms in history from 1896 to 1899. Many of the mines faded away in the years to come, except a number of larger mines which continued to produce handsomely, although sporadically—there was actually no continuous producer until 1936.

Here is where the tremendous Knob Hill mine enters the picture. Discovered by W.H. "Billy" Kells in 1897, it is known as the biggest and most consistent producer of gold and silver in the history of the Republic Mining District. An on-site, ore mill was constructed in 1936. A power line was brought in from Tonasket, 40 miles away, to provide power for both the mill and the town of Republic. In the following years the Knob Hill mine was thought to be worked out on more than one occasion, but in 1965 it celebrated 29 years of continuous operation. In 1975 the Knob Hill mine was said to be the only gold mine operating in Ferry County. Finally, mining was terminated February 28, 1978 after 44 years of continuous operation. However, by July 31, 1978, after some rehabilitation, the mine was back in operation with some 50 men at work. In the mid 1980s the Knob Hill mine was again facing possible closure (for a third time).

Around this time the company gambled 500,000 dollars on a geologist's hunch and won—two new ore veins were located and named the Golden Promise numbers 1 and 2. The Golden Promise, along with its 2.2 million-dollar, 1,300-foot-deep vertical shaft, was dedicated in late December of 1986. Over 70,000 ounces of gold was produced from the Golden Promise mine in 1987; and from 1988-1993, 556,838 tons of ore was milled producing 430,455 ounces of gold and 1,893,214 ounces of silver.

In the mid 1980s when the Knob Hill mine announced possible closure, it was decided by town leaders that Republic should no longer depend primarily on the mine for economic stability. As a result, Republic has changed in recent years. False fronts on many of the 1900s vintage buildings along the main street (historic Clark Avenue) have been modified to provide a more rustic appeal for tourists. It is hoped that the area's history, beautiful scenery, and recreational opportunities will bring more outside money to the town.

It was announced by the Hecla Mining Company in October of 1994 that the Republic Unit mine (the historic Knob Hill and Golden Promise mines) will be starting closure January 2, 1995. Exploration efforts, however, are being continued, and the hope is that a new ore body will be discovered. Republic now faces some hard times, and one can only hope and pray that another "Golden Promise" will soon become reality.

Blue Lake in the Sinlahekin Valley.

Region 2

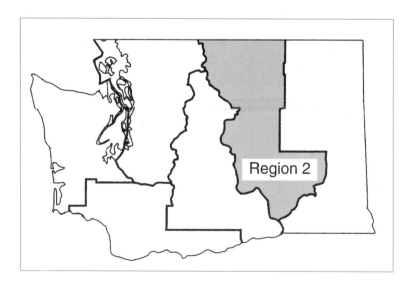

Region 2

Chopaka Lake

	106	107	108	109	110	111	112	113	114	115	116	117	118	119
90	91	92	93	94	95	96	97	98	99	100	101	102	103	104	105
74	75	76	77	78	79	80	81	82	83	84	85	86	87	88	89
58	59	60	61	62	63	64	65	66	67	68	69	70	71	72	73
	58	44	45	46	47	48	49	50	51	52	53	54	55	56	57
	58	30	31	32	33	34	35	36	37	38	39	40	41	42	43
			22	23	24	25	26	27	28	29				

Washington Atlas & Gazetteer Mapping Grid

Chopaka Lake is located in Okanogan County (T39N R25E S4 and T40N R25E S33), 6.5 miles northwest of Loomis and 5 miles south of the Canada/U.S. border. (See *Washington Atlas and Gazetteer* pg. 114, A-3 and U.S.G.S. Nighthawk.) [SPECIAL REGULATIONS]

Chopaka Lake lies 2,921 feet above sea level in the picturesque Okanogan Mountains. It covers 160 surface acres with a maximum depth of 73 feet and mean depth of 23 feet. Chopaka Lake is well known for its hard-fighting fish, abundant mayfly (*Callibaetis*) population, and outstanding dry fly fishing. It is very popular with fly anglers—almost too popular. I have seen the entire campground and parking area packed with people and vehicles; even a simple task such as finding a place to park was difficult! The lake is 1.5 miles long, and sheltered between high, partially timbered ridges. Lush, grassy meadows that are characteristic of the Okanogan Mountains surround much of the shoreline. The northwest base of 3,700-foot Grandview Mountain rises from the east shore and the southeast base of 7,800-foot Chopaka Mountain rises from the west shore. The only nearshore development is a public campground along the west central part of the lake.

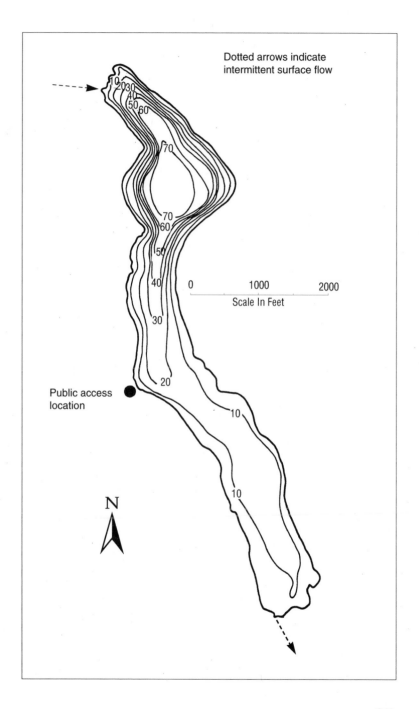

Dotted arrows indicate
intermittent surface flow

10 20 30
40
50 60

70

70
60

50

40

30

20

0   1000   2000
Scale In Feet

Public access
location

10

10

N

Chopaka Lake.

The lake's south half is shallow, almost entirely under 15 feet in depth, with submersed aquatic weeds covering large portions of the lake bottom. Reeds cover most of its shoreline. The south half is by far the most heavily fished area of the lake. The north half, on the other hand, has a much steeper bottom slope, and submersed weed growth is limited to scattered areas along the narrow littoral bottom. Reeds cover about half of the shoreline area. The north half receives far less fishing pressure. (This not due to a lack of good fishing!) Chopaka Lake is fed primarily by groundwater seepage. A small spring-fed stream flows into the north end during wet years. Intermittent surface drainage is southward to Chopaka Creek which follows a small quaking aspen-lined draw through beautiful rangeland dotted with grazing cattle. The area has abundant populations of big game such as mule and white-tailed deer, black bear, and bighorn sheep. On two occasions I have seen a black bear slowly eat its way across meadows above the lake and disappear into the timber.

Rainbow trout in Chopaka Lake are strong, and very well-conditioned. They have a knack for making long runs and diving into weeds. Great care must be taken when using light tippets as they can be difficult to handle. Most fish will be 12-18 inches with larger fish available. The shallows are packed with all kinds of aquatic trout foods, particularly scuds, mayflies, and damselflies. Fishing the mayfly hatch is very popular at Chopaka Lake. A fly angler can imitate rising nymphs and emergers in the morning hours until around mid-day when the duns hatch and dry their wings on the surface. This mid-day period can provide outstanding dry-fly fishing. The mayfly spinner fall usually comes on in late afternoon. Watch for these times of excellent surface action.

Access to Chopaka Lake is relatively rough and requires some serious climbing. From Highway 97 in Tonasket, turn west at the Loomis/Nighthawk recreation sign and drive 1/3 mile to a T-intersection (Loomis-Oroville Road). Turn right and head north then west on the Loomis-Oroville Road for 19.4 miles, passing through the town of Loomis, to the signed turnoff for Chopaka Lake in the Sinlahekin Valley. Turn left and drive 1.4 miles to where a gravel road branches off to the right. This is where the steep, relatively rough, mountain road begins—the first 2 miles climb at a very steep grade, requiring both patience and low gear the whole way. Coming down can be hard on the brakes, especially with a trailer. Despite its steep grade and rough washboard, the road provides an incredible birds-eye view of the Sinlahekin Valley and Palmer Lake. From the beginning of the steep mountain road, climb for 5.1 miles, staying on the main road, to a Y-intersection. Take the right branch and descend about 2 miles to the campground and access area on the west central shore of Chopaka Lake.

Loomis

Six-and-a-half miles southeast of Chopaka Lake is the quiet community of Loomis where a small handful of people still reside. The first settlers came to the area in the early 1870s and operated a large cattle venture owned by the Yakima firm, Phelps and Wadleigh. Chief Moses was paid for grazing rights. In the bitter winter of 1879-80 their entire herd of 3,000 cattle perished. This wiped out the enterprise.

About this time J.A. Loomis, an early rancher who gave the town its name, started what would later become a business partnership for himself. He noticed that neighboring ranchers would run out of supplies before new shipments came in. So, he stored up extra supplies for himself, and when his neighbors ran out he would let them have his extra supplies for cost. In 1884 an easterner named Guy Waring came to Loomis with his wife and 3 young stepchildren. Waring purchased cattle and became an Okanogan rancher—he lasted 3 years. During this period he also started a general store in his house and took on J.A. Loomis as a partner. The store grew into the largest business in town and not only served local ranchers and homesteaders, but also miners who had come to the area in the 1870s after experiencing discouragement in the Fraser River mining camps of British Columbia. (The area legally opened to homesteading in 1886 when the Moses-Columbia Reservation was removed. The reservation had been established in 1879 and extended eastward from the west bank of the Okanogan River to the Cascade crest, and northward from the mouth of the Okanogan River to British Columbia.)

After 3 years in the Loomis area, Guy Waring sold out and returned with his family to Boston. In his book *My Pioneer Past*, Waring explains this action by saying, "The social formalities of civilization die hard in a woman's mind." However, Waring and his family returned to Washington state in 1891 and began a trading company on the Methow River. (See Winthrop after Big Twin Lake for further information about Guy Waring.)

Loomis grew quickly in the following years on the area's economic base of mining, logging, ranching, and farming. Loomis had the usual business and entertainment services of towns during this era. The rich mining strikes (first placer gold rush and first lode gold discovery in the state) on which the town mushroomed were short-lived and the town slowly declined. The last ores were taken from nearby Palmer Mountain in 1927. (The Grand Summit Mine on Palmer Mountain was unbelievably rich in the early days. It had assays of nearly 1,900 ounces of gold per ton of ore!) This was the final chapter in the demise of Loomis as a going town.

Sidley Lake

Sidley Lake is located in Okanogan County (T40N R29E S6), 10 miles northeast of Oroville and .5 mile south of the Canada/U.S. border. (See *Washington Atlas and Gazetteer* pg. 115, A-7 and U.S.G.S. Molson.)

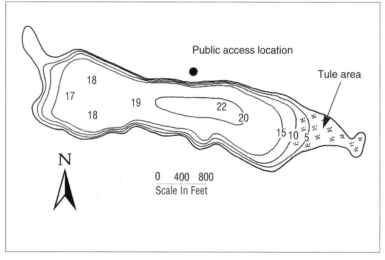

Washington Atlas & Gazetteer Mapping Grid

At an altitude of 3,660 feet, Sidley Lake covers 120 surface acres with a maximum depth of 22 feet and mean depth of 15 feet. Sidley Lake is situated among rolling meadows and partially timbered ridges of the beautiful Okanogan Highlands. Big game is abundant in the area with mule and white-tailed deer, black bear, and bighorn sheep. Its setting is tranquil and pastoral, characteristic of the entire Okanogan Highland farm and ranch country. Several homes are scattered along the northwest and southwest shorelines. The Sidley Lake Resort was started at the lake's northwest corner in 1961. The place changed hands in 1973 and continued operation until it closed in

Sidley Lake.

1986. The northwest corner also houses an aerator machine to help prevent winter kill by raising dissolved oxygen levels. The aerator was installed in 1979 and is maintained by the North Okanogan County Sportsman's Club.

Sidley is a rich, productive lake with fast-growing rainbow trout and an abundance of aquatic food sources that include damselflies, dragonflies, caddisflies, mayflies, leeches, scuds, snails, and midges. It contains a very large population of zooplankton and has a high algal density. The littoral bottom is a reddish brown silty muck, covered in many areas by a short carpeting of sphagnum moss. Other varieties of submersed weed growth are very limited, almost non-existent. Reeds cover much of the shoreline and choke a good portion of the shallow bay at the east end of the lake. The south shore is littered with logs and wood debris; the north shore is primarily road fill. Sidley Lake has no surface inlet or outlet; it is fed and drained entirely by ground-water seepage. The east and west ends have the most extensive shallows. The rest of the lake drops quickly to 15 feet in depth and then flattens out to form an extensive, relatively shallow (15-20 feet) bottom area. The lake is well circulated with high levels of dissolved oxygen throughout the water column.

Rainbow trout in Sidley Lake are well-conditioned. They average 12-16 inches with larger fish to 20-plus inches. The fish are active fighters and can really take line off the reel when they are in the mood. I clearly recall a couple of times when the occasional "big fish" bolted into my backing. Lahontan cutthroat have also been stocked in past years.

Sidley is an excellent lake but has one unfortunate disadvantage—standard harvest regulations. Numerous bait and hardware-trolling anglers fish Sidley Lake year-round and harvest a large number of fish. With special regulations limiting fish harvest, prohibiting bait fishing, and promoting catch and release, Sidley would produce a much greater number of holdovers in the 16- to 20-inch range.

To reach Sidley Lake from Highway 97 in Oroville, turn east on Central Avenue at the sign for Sidley Lake and Molson. Drive 1/3 mile to Cherry Street, turn left on Cherry, continuing to follow signs for Molson. Go 2/3 mile on Cherry, turn right on Oroville-Toroda Road, and drive east out of town for 9.9 miles to the signed turnoff for Molson. Turn north on Molson Road and drive 6.5 miles, passing through Molson, to the northeast end of Sidley Lake. The road borders the entire north shore of the lake.

Molson

Less than 1 mile southeast of Sidley Lake in the pastoral Okanogan Highlands lies the ghost town of Molson. About 1/2 mile south of town and just off Molson Road lies the Old Molson Museum—original townsite of Molson.

The Story of Molson

Molson was founded in April of 1900 when promoter George B. Meacham interested the Molson family of Montreal, Canada in a mining and townsite enterprise. The Molsons were a prominent family who owned the Molson Bank of Canada, with branches in every province, and also operated the largest brewing company in Canada. George Meacham, as general manager of the enterprise, began to build a town. A number of mining claims were staked nearby, the townsite was organized (it had 40 blocks with a main street that was 100 feet wide), and within a short time several businesses flourished, including the 3-story Hotel Tonasket named after the Okanogan chief. Meacham spent 50,000 dollars of company money, including 8,100 dollars for the Hotel Tonasket. Hotel Tonasket sported a 2-story outhouse, bar, dining room, and 34 guest rooms. However, in February of 1901 the Molson family withdrew its financial backing due to a lack of promise in mining prospects. (The Poland China on upper Mary Ann Creek was the only mine in the area to ship ore.) The town's population fell from 300 to less than a dozen in 1901. The Hotel Tonasket and several other businesses survived for a few years until the town again boomed with construction of the railroad and arrival of homesteaders. Homesteaders were drawn by the fact that in 1900 the northern half of the Colville Indian Reservation, which then included the Molson area, had been opened to homestead and timber claims. Before then, as of 1896, mining claims were only allowed.

During this time a farmer named John H. McDonald, who owned the town's livery barn and a stagecoach line, filed on a homestead which he claimed included the Molson townsite. When promoter George Meacham started the town he had squatter's rights but never filed a plat. (Squatter's rights, a de facto first-come, first-served claim, was valid as long as the claimant was not absent from the land for longer than 6 months at a time.) John McDonald was aware of this and took advantage of a newly completed land survey when he filed his homestead. This began a controversy and legal battle (Government Townsite versus J.H. McDonald) that lasted nearly twenty years. When the railroad company came to Molson around 1905 they decided to build their depot about 1/2 mile north of town (because of J.H. McDonald). The Molson railroad depot was the highest in the state at an altitude of 3,708 feet. When it became evident that clear land titles could not be obtained in Molson, a couple of its enraged citizens, Watkins W. Parry and Noah LaCasse, founded the town of New Molson in 1905 on Noah LaCasse's land near the railroad depot. Here Watkins Parry built a large general store. They set an example that many Old Molson residents would soon follow. (Before Watkins W. Perry came to Molson, he had opened a store at Tonasket in 1888 and built a ferry there in 1895 on the Okanogan River for use when the river was at flood stages.)

Both New and Old Molson prospered in the ensuing years. Old Molson had a post office, bank, the Molson Magnate newspaper, 3 general stores, furniture store, lumber yard, automobile and agricultural implement dealership, real estate and homestead locating business, millinery shop, an attorney, schoolhouse, a doctor and drug store, barber shop, 3 saloons, dance hall, livery barn, blacksmith shop and harness maker, assay office, and the Hotel Tonasket. However, the J.H. McDonald land dispute continued to rage. By the time it was finally settled around 1920, most Old Molson citizens and businesses (including the post office) had moved away in disgust to New Molson, leaving Old Molson a ghost town. (Hotel Tonasket was destroyed by fire in May, 1923.)

With the influx of Old Molson residents adding to the many businesses already established, New Molson boomed and grew into the commercial center of the Okanogan Highlands with a peak population of 700! Its trading area reached from 20 miles south to 10 miles into Canada, and in its prime was the largest railroad freight shipper from Oroville to Spokane. New Molson had everything one could imagine from movie theaters and automobile dealerships (125 cars were sold in 1917), to churches, masonic lodges, and a 12-year school (now preserved as a museum). This affluence was short lived, however, as the Great Depression took its toll. The railroad tracks were removed by 1935, businesses and homes were destroyed by fire, and many residents left the dying Molson to a better life in booming Oroville.

Many of the old buildings have long since vanished into history, and the former glory days are just a memory. The one thing that remains constant, however, is the timeless beauty of the Okanogan Highlands.

Old Molson Museum

The Old Molson Museum has an interesting collection of antique buildings, household relics, farm and ranch implements, mining implements, and logging implements. These relics were gathered from all over the Highlands and some from Oroville and Tonasket. The Museum is open anytime and designed for people who enjoy browsing around the grounds and inside the buildings to see a piece of interesting local history.

Many of the old buildings and relics were donated by local individuals and moved from nearby locations to the present site from 1963-1974. The only original building at the site was the Old Molson State Bank. Several of the buildings were in poor shape and had to be restored. Harry Sherling, who grew up 1.5 miles north of Old Molson from 1902 to 1920 in the Sherling family homestead cabin, had a vision to see the site of Old Molson restored and preserved for history—a place where former residents could once again see the horse-age equipment and relics with which they were so familiar. He spearheaded the project, with assistance from the Okanogan County Historical Society, and is responsible for much of what is now the Old Molson Museum. Buildings at the site include the Sherling family cabin (1902), homestead cabin of Severt O. Rise (1908), Bill Stewart's saloon (1900), Barney Fletcher's old shingle mill (1904), Law of the Highlands—Charles Dvorak, attorney (1909-1910), Walker and O'Dell—homestead locaters (1900-1906), Poland China and Molson gold mine assay office (1896), and the Molson State Bank (1912-1917).

If you decide to fish Sidley Lake sometime or find yourself near the Okanogan Highlands, head up to Molson and visit the Old Molson Museum. It is certainly a worthwhile experience.

Proctor Lake

Note: Proctor Lake depends on state fish plants of fingerlings and private granting of access. It is best to check ahead to make sure the lake is open. Call Region 2 office of the Washington Department of Fish and Wildlife.

Proctor Lake is located in Okanogan County (T34N R26E S11), 3.5 miles north of Omak on the Bide-A-Wee Flat. Proctor Lake is 500 feet north of Duck Lake. (See *Washington Atlas and Gazetteer* pg. 100, A-4 and U.S.G.S. Omak.) [SPECIAL REGULATIONS]

Proctor Lake covers 7 surface acres at high water and lies at an altitude of 1,240 feet. Maximum depth is 39 feet with a mean depth of 22 feet. The lake stage varies with the water table, changing depth and acreage. The lake level has been low for several years due to recent drought conditions. Proctor is situated in a glacial kettle basin surrounded by a short, steep, grass and sage-covered rim. Proctor Lake has the steep bottom slope that is characteristic of many glacial kettles.

Glacial Kettle Formation Theory—Glacial kettles were formed in northern North America as the continental ice sheet retreated. During this process, the great glaciers left behind expansive plains of meltwater outwash (glacially transported debris composed of sand and gravel sediments, deposited over extensive areas beyond the ice front by powerful meltwater streams). These outwash plains often contained very large segments of ice broken from the decaying glaci-

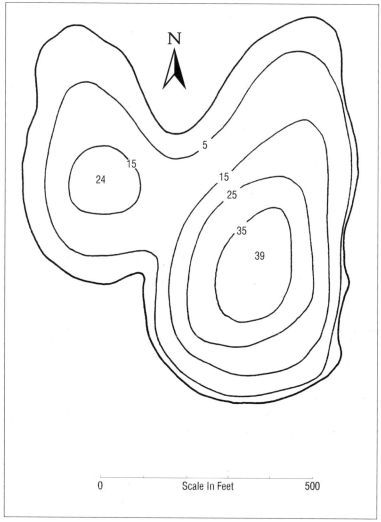

er. The great, buried ice blocks melted over a period of many years, leaving behind numerous basins in the outwash debris. This resulted in the formation of thousands of small kettle lakes.

Proctor Lake, known as Goose Lake in the 1920s, is a very personal, little lake situated in the midst of farm and ranch country. It is sheltered in its small basin and protected from much of the wind. Surrounding views are of peaks in the Okanogan high country to the

Proctor Lake.

northwest, orchards, sage flats, and sparsely timbered ridges covered with sagebrush and grass. Sparse reed growth covers most of the shoreline and the littoral bottom is covered with a light growth of thin, slime-like vegetation. Proctor Lake has no inlet or outlet streams; it is fed and drained entirely by groundwater seepage. Insects are abundant with many of the usual critters, including scuds. This aquatic life, however, seems to run a bit on the small side.

Proctor Lake grows beautiful, well-conditioned rainbow trout. Average size is 12-16 inches with larger fish to 20 inches. Eastern brook trout have also been stocked in past years.

To reach Proctor Lake from Highway 97 at Omak, turn west at the North Omak exit onto Riverside Drive. Go west for .8 mile to Ross Canyon Road. Head north then west on Ross Canyon Road for .7 mile to Duck Lake Road. Turn north on Duck Lake Road and drive for 2.6 miles to Duck Lake and the public access turnoff. Park at Duck Lake (also a kettle lake) and walk northerly along Duck's east shore for just under 1/2 mile to the south side of Proctor Lake. Keep a sharp lookout for rattlesnakes.

Blue Lake

	106	107	108	109	110	111	112	113	114	115	116	117	118	119
90	91	92	93	94	95	96	97	98	99	100	101	102	103	104	105
74	75	76	77	78	79	80	81	82	83	84	85	86	87	88	89
58	59	60	61	62	63	64	65	66	67	68	69	70	71	72	73
	58	44	45	46	47	48	49	50	51	52	53	54	55	56	57
	58	30	31	32	33	34	35	36	37	38	39	40	41	42	43
			22	23	24	25	26	27	28	29					

Washington Atlas & Gazetteer Mapping Grid

Blue Lake is located in Okanogan County (T39N R27E S6 and T39N R26E S1), 3 miles southwest of Oroville above the Okanogan Valley. (See *Washington Atlas and Gazetteer* pg. 115, A-5 and U.S.G.S. Oroville.) [SPECIAL REGULATIONS]

Blue Lake covers 112 surface acres and lies at an altitude of 1,783 feet. Maximum depth is 114 feet with a mean depth of 64 feet. The lake is situated in a rangeland basin, surrounded by high, rugged hills covered with grass and sagebrush. Grazing cattle are scattered throughout the area. Several sheer, rock walls border the lake, especially at the west side. These cliffs are popular with local dare-devils who enjoy the thrill of leaping to the water far below.

Blue Lake has high alkaline water and for many years could not support fish life—not until the Lahontan cutthroat. Lahontan cutthroat can survive and thrive in high alkaline water and have created outstanding fisheries out of many barren lakes. The water level varies several feet each year, changing the depth and acreage slightly. Lower water levels expose an underwater bedrock upthrust in the southeast section of the lake, forming two very small islands. An intermittent runoff stream flows into the west central side of the lake; there is no

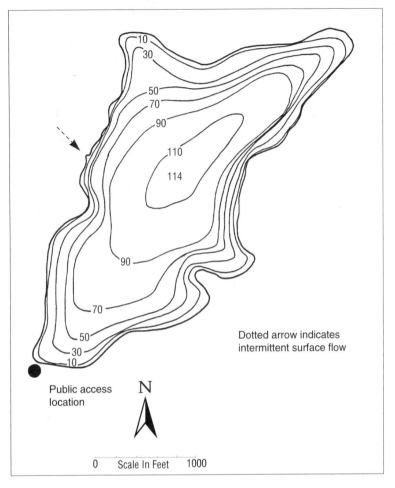

110

114

90

70

50

30

10

Dotted arrow indicates
intermittent surface flow

Public access
location

N

0   Scale In Feet   1000

surface outflow. Blue Lake has a steep bottom slope with a very limit-ed littoral area. Large portions of the shallows are covered with a heavy growth of submersed aquatic weeds. A very thick muck covers the lake bottom, making any kind of wading impossible—one can sink waist-deep in the blink of an eye!

Lahontan cutthroat in Blue Lake feed on the lake's abundant insect populations and grow to large sizes. They average 16-20 inches with larger fish to 6 pounds or better. I have had good success early and late in the day near the submerged, bedrock upthrust in the

Blue Lake.

southeast part of the lake. Lahontan cutthroat are different in some ways from rainbow trout. For one, they seem to feed with less surface rises. Also, they do not fight in quite the same manner, preferring to "log it out" below the surface. Occasionally they make a strong run, and very rarely will they leap out of the water. Many anglers claim that they are more bold than a rainbow and not as easily spooked. There are times when big Lahontans will even follow a boat and swim along-side of it. They are also very territorial, striking an irritating fly or lure more out of aggression than anything else.

To reach Blue Lake from Highway 97 in Oroville (main street), turn west at the sign for Wannacut Lake and drive 1 mile to the next sign for Wannacut Lake. Turn right and drive 1.7 miles, bearing south-ward on Golden Road, to the signed turnoff for both Wannacut and Blue lakes. Turn west on Blue Lake Road and go 2.5 miles on gravel road to the public access turnoff at the lake's southwest corner. The gravel road borders the southeast shoreline.

Ell Lake

		106	107	108	109	110	111	112	113	114	115	116	117	118	119
90	91	92	93	94	95	96	97	98	99	100	101	102	103	104	105
74	75	76	77	78	79	80	81	82	83	84	85	86	87	88	89
58	59	60	61	62	63	64	65	66	67	68	69	70	71	72	73
	58	44	45	46	47	48	49	50	51	52	53	54	55	56	57
	58	30	31	32	33	34	35	36	37	38	39	40	41	42	43
			22	23	24	25	26	27	28	29					

Washington Atlas & Gazetteer Mapping Grid

Ell Lake, also called "L" Lake, is located in Okanogan County (T36N R30E S19), 16 miles southeast of Tonasket in the beautiful Aeneas Valley of the Okanogan Highlands. (See *Washington Atlas and Gazetteer* pg. 115, D-8 and U.S.G.S. Tunk Mountain and Bailey Creek.) [SPECIAL REGULATIONS]

Ell Lake covers 24 surface acres at high water and lies at an altitude of 2,592 feet. Maximum depth at high water is 19 feet with a mean depth of 12 feet. The lake level fluctuates several feet and can get quite low during years of dry weather. Some water is also pumped from the lake for minor irrigation. Ell Lake is situated in a small glacial kettle basin. (See Proctor Lake for a description of glacial kettle formation.) Partially timbered mountain ridges with expansive grassy meadows flank both sides of the Aeneas Valley. Views to the northeast are of 6,051-foot Mt. Annie; 4,800-foot Mt. Sneed rises to the southeast. Several small homes sit on the grass and sage-covered kettle rim above the lake.

Ell Lake is fed primarily by groundwater seepage; an intermittent stream (Edwards Creek) flows into the northwest end of the lake. Drainage takes place through underground seepage as there is no

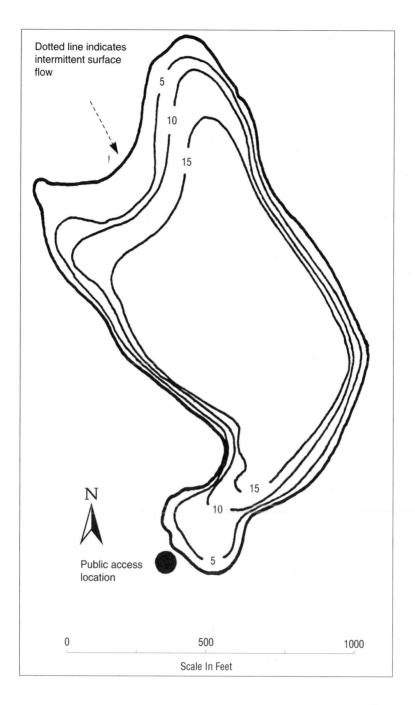

Dotted line indicates intermittent surface flow

5

10

15

N

15

10

5

Public access location

0   500   1000

Scale In Feet

surface outlet. The northeast and southwest sides of the lake have steep bottom slopes that drop quickly into 10-15 feet of water (depending on lake level). The entire lake bottom is covered with a heavy growth of submersed aquatic vegetation. Some of the slender weeds and grasses grow very tall in places, and at certain times of year they can choke large areas of the lake. Because of this, it is particularly important to give the fly frequent physical examinations. Small pieces of grass and weeds can very easily attach to the hook without the angler realizing it. I never recall having good luck fishing with a weedy hook.

Ell Lake is crammed with aquatic trout foods, especially scuds, damselflies, dragonflies, and mayflies. With this available feed, rainbow trout in Ell Lake grow very quickly and are full of vitality. Most fish will be 12-18 inches with occasional larger trout to a little over 20 inches. Ell Lake provides some outstanding dry fly fishing at times.

From Highway 97 at the south end of Tonasket, drive east on Highway 20 toward Republic for 13.1 miles to Aeneas Valley Road. Go southeast on Aeneas Valley Road for 6 miles to the public fishing access turnoff for Ell Lake. Parking and launch area is at the south end of the lake. Low water levels have left the boat ramp high and dry since the mid 1980s due to drought conditions throughout the area. The water level has improved some very recently and hopefully will raise once again to its former level.

Aeneas Valley

The Aeneas Valley (Ee-nee-us), where Ell Lake is situated, is named after an Okanogan chief who claimed and settled the entire 15 mile-long valley in 1863. He came to the valley with his family and livestock and raised cattle, horses, and oats until the late 1880s. His right to claim the entire valley was not contested up to this time until white ranchers came and filed claims, and new laws reduced his property to 160 acres. He lived here in the valley until his death in 1905. When Chief Aeneas first came to the valley in 1863, it was at the expense of leaving both his ancestral lands west of the Okanogan River and his role as Okanogan chief. Young men in his tribe felt it was necessary to kill invading white miners and settlers. Chief Aeneas knew this was futile, but was unable to control the young men. He then moved away and settled in the beautiful, grassy valley that one day would bear his name.

Big Twin Lake

	106	107	108	109	110	111	112	113	114	115	116	117	118	119
90	91	92	93	94	95	96	97	98	99 ■	100	101	102	103	104	105
74	75	76	77	78	79	80	81	82	83	84	85	86	87	88	89
58	59	60	61	62	63	64	65	66	67	68	69	70	71	72	73
	58	44	45	46	47	48	49	50	51	52	53	54	55	56	57
	58	30	31	32	33	34	35	36	37	38	39	40	41	42	43
			22	23	24	25	26	27	28	29				

Washington Atlas &
Gazetteer Mapping
Grid

Big Twin Lake is located in Okanogan County (T34N R21E S15), 2 miles south of Winthrop. It is situated in the heart of the beautiful Methow River Valley on the east edge of the spectacular North Cascade Range. (See *Washington Atlas and Gazetteer* pg. 99, A-7 and U.S.G.S. Winthrop.) [SPECIAL REGULATIONS]

The lake lies at an altitude of 1,799 feet and covers 79 surface acres. Maximum depth is 70 feet with a mean depth of 24 feet. Big Twin Lake lies in a glacial kettle basin in a semi-agricultural area. The setting is very attractive with surrounding views of mountain ridges; Blue Buck Mountain to the east, Pearrygin and Tripod peaks to the northeast, jagged 8,000-foot peaks of the eastern North Cascades far to the north, and Patterson Mountain rising above the lake's west side. Big Twin Lake has a steep overall bottom slope that is characteristic of many glacial kettle lakes. (See Proctor Lake for a description of glacial kettle formation.) There is no surface water inflow or outflow; the lake is fed and drained entirely by underground seepage. Water level varies some during the course of a year, especially during years of dry weather. A large portion of the shoreline is covered by reeds and over half of the lake bottom is covered with submersed weed

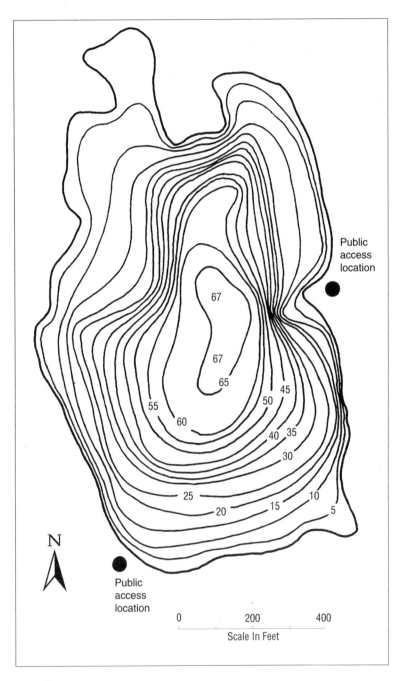

Public
access
location

N

Public
access
location

0   200   400
Scale In Feet

Big Twin Lake.

growth to depths of 20 or more feet. Several homes sit on the grassy, pine and sage-covered rim surrounding the lake. The Big Twin Lake Campground is located at the lake's northwest corner.

Rainbow and Lahontan cutthroat trout in Big Twin Lake have an abundance of aquatic foods, including scuds, to feast on resulting in very strong, well-conditioned fish. Rainbows usually average 12-18 inches and Lahontans will be in the 18- to 22-inch range. One of my most memorable experiences at Big Twin Lake came in late October of the 1993 season. After a windy, fairly slow day of fishing that produced two reel-screaming hits, I decided to wait out the afternoon and tackle the lake at sunset. After the sun disappeared behind Patterson Mountain, I kicked my float tube over to the lake's northeast section, armed with a black mini-leech and 4-weight intermediate line. Within 10 minutes I released a 4-pound Lahontan cutthroat. Several minutes later a 2-pound rainbow bolted 20 yards into the backing. The next hour-and-a-half was filled with one strong rainbow after another—not a single fish failed to reach the backing. I went to bed completely worn out and laughing. A rare experience, no doubt, but great while it lasted!

Access for Big Twin Lake is from Winthrop on Highway 20. Turn on Twin Lakes Road at the southeast edge of town, just on the south side of the Methow River Bridge. Drive 2.9 miles on Twin Lakes Road to the Big Twin Lake Campground and RV Park turnoff; continue another 1/2 mile to the public fishing access turnoff for the lake's south end; continue another 1/2 mile to the public access turnoff for the lake's east side and turn north, driving about 1/2 mile on a gravel road to the lake.

Winthrop

Winthrop, 2 miles north of Big Twin Lake, is a reconstructed frontier-style town, popular today with many tourists. Several of the present buildings, altered though they are, actually remain from Winthrop's earlier days.

Winthrop began shortly after 1891 when Guy Waring, a Harvard graduate and classmate of Theodore Roosevelt, began a trading post on the Methow River to provide needed items for local ranchers and miners. Waring soon had branch outlets of his trading company in Twisp, Pateros, and the mining camps of Robinson and Barron. Waring also built the Duck Brand Saloon, named for his cattle brand, at Winthrop in 1895. It is somewhat surprising that Waring built and operated a saloon since he had a hatred for liquor. It is easier to make sense of his actions, however, knowing that he believed the best way to prevent intoxication was to control the sale of liquor—and he served only the finest whiskey. Around 1897 Waring built the comfortable home he had promised his wife. It was a log structure known as The Castle, constructed with great attention to detail.

The building originally occupied by the Duck Brand Saloon became the Winthrop Hotel in 1908. A few years later the same building was leased as a hospital; when the doctor left town the building once again became the Winthrop Hotel. This structural "hot potato" is today's community center and library. Guy Waring's home, The Castle, is now the Shafter Museum. The Shafter Museum is named after a local man who purchased the house and used it to display his collection of antique equipment and implements used by pioneers. Also, Waring's Methow Trading Post originally occupied the building now called Last Trading Post.

Blue Lake

Blue Lake is located in Okanogan County (T37N R25E S21,22,27,28), 9 miles south of Loomis and 12 miles west of

	106	107	108	109	110	111	112	113	114	115	116	117	118	119
90	91	92	93	94	95	96	97	98	99	100	101	102	103	104	105
74	75	76	77	78	79	80	81	82	83	84	85	86	87	88	89
58	59	60	61	62	63	64	65	66	67	68	69	70	71	72	73
	59	44	45	46	47	48	49	50	51	52	53	54	55	56	57
	58	30	31	32	33	34	35	36	37	38	39	40	41	42	43
			22	23	24	25	26	27	28	29				

Washington Atlas & Gazetteer Mapping Grid

Tonasket at the head of the Sinlahekin Valley. Blue Lake is part of the 14,000-acre Sinlahekin Wildlife Area. (See *Washington Atlas and Gazetteer* pg. 114, C-3 and U.S.G.S. Blue Goat Mountain.) [SPECIAL REGULATIONS]

At an altitude of 1,686 feet, Blue Lake covers 160 surface acres. Maximum depth is 69 feet with a mean depth of 28 feet. In 1923 a small dam was constructed to form present-day Blue Lake, inundating 3 natural lakes: original Blue Lake (north arm), Long Lake (south arm), and Round Lake (extreme south end). They were called "Three Pools" in 1887. Blue is a long lake situated between steep mountain ridges of the beautiful Sinlahekin Valley. 5,054-foot Blue Goat Mountain rises from the lake's west shore. 5,350-foot Twin Peaks rise to the northwest. Big game such as mule and white-tailed deer, black bear, and bighorn sheep are abundant in the area. An alert observer can occasionally see bighorn sheep negotiating sheer, rocky inclines of the surrounding ridges.

Sloping, grassy meadows surround the lake's shoreline which is covered mostly with brush and small trees; reed growth is scattered and covers about 1/3 of the shoreline. Blue Lake is partially fed by groundwater seepage; a small, intermittent runoff stream also flows off Blue Goat Mountain into the northwest corner of the lake. An outlet stream flows northerly to Sinlahekin Creek. Submersed weed growth covers scattered portions of the littoral

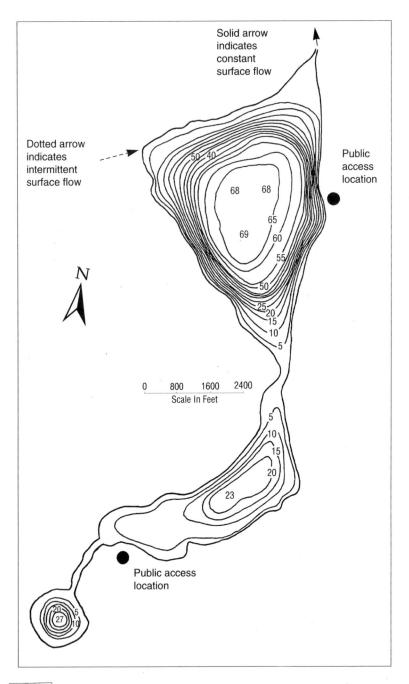

Solid arrow indicates constant surface flow

Dotted arrow indicates intermittent surface flow

Public access location

N

50 40
68 68
65
69 60
55
50
25 20
15
10
5

0   800   1600   2400
Scale In Feet

5
10
15
20
23

Public access location

20 5
27 10

Blue Goat Mountain above Blue Lake.

bottom, particularly along gradually-sloping areas. The littoral bottom is mostly muck.

Blue Lake has a good population of aquatic trout foods, including scuds, and a good number of redside shiners. These shiners compete for available feed with the rainbow trout, and hinder their growth rate. However, rainbows that feed heavily on these shiners can grow quickly to large proportions. Fish typically average 12-16 inches with larger, elusive fish to 20-plus inches. On several occasions I have fished with small, minnow imitations. They seem to work well in Blue Lake, particularly for big fish.

From Highway 97 about 5.5 miles north of Riverside, turn west on Pine Creek Road toward Conconully and the Sinlahekin Valley. Drive 13.8 miles on Pine Creek Road (after 8 miles it turns into Fish Lake Road and becomes gravel; after passing Fish Lake the road turns north and becomes Sinlahekin Road) to the south end public access and camping area for Blue Lake. Additional access and camping areas are available at the north arm of Blue Lake.

Aeneas Lake

		106	107	108	109	110	111	112	113	114	115	116	117	118	119
90	91	92	93	94	95	96	97	98	99	100	101	102	103	104	105
74	75	76	77	78	79	80	81	82	83	84	85	86	87	88	89
58	59	60	61	62	63	64	65	66	67	68	69	70	71	72	73
	58	44	45	46	47	48	49	50	51	52	53	54	55	56	57
	58	30	31	32	33	34	35	36	37	38	39	40	41	42	43
			22	23	24	25	26	27	28	29					

Washington Atlas & Gazetteer Mapping Grid

Aeneas Lake is located in Okanogan County (T37N R26E S25), about 4 miles southwest of Tonasket above the Okanogan Valley. (See *Washington Atlas and Gazetteer* pg. 114, C-4 and U.S.G.S. Aeneas Lake.) [SPECIAL REGULATIONS]

Aeneas Lake (Ee-nee-us) is named for an Okanogan chief who moved away from his ancestral lands west of the Okanogan River to settle in the Aeneas Valley of the Okanogan Highlands in 1863. Aeneas Lake lies in a glacial kettle basin at an altitude of 1,380 feet. It covers 62 surface acres with a maximum depth of 62 feet and mean depth of 29 feet. The overall bottom slope is steep, characteristic once again of a glacial kettle basin. (See Proctor Lake for a description of glacial kettle formation.) The north end has the lake's most extensive shallow water area and the heaviest growth of submersed aquatic vegetation. Gradual, shallow areas around other parts of the lake also have a good growth of submersed vegetation. There are some small springs in the lake around which fish gather. If an angler can find these areas of seepage, fishing may be outstanding. An intermittent inflow from Horse Springs Coulee comes in at the lake's northwest corner; there is no outlet channel.

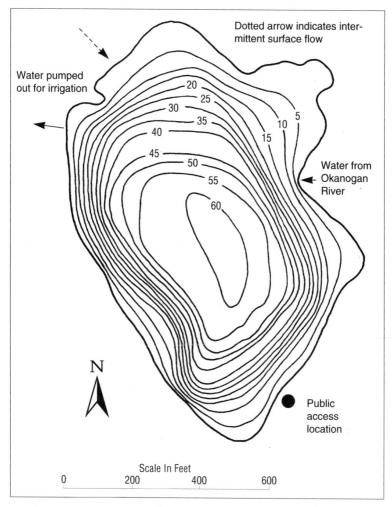

Dotted arrow indicates intermittent surface flow

Water pumped out for irrigation

Water from Okanogan River

Public access location

N

Scale In Feet
0   200   400   600

Aeneas Lake is situated in an agricultural basin surrounded by rugged, sage and grass-covered hills. Partially timbered mountain ridges provide a backdrop to the northwest. 5,167-foot Lemansky Mountain with a lookout perched on its crest draws the eye of an observer to the northwest. An orchard borders the entire west shoreline. The orchard has rights to pump water from Aeneas Lake for irrigation; large pipes extend into the northwest section of the lake. To prevent a significant drop in the lake level from this orchard pumping, water is transported from the Okanogan River, 2 miles away, to replenish the water pumped out by the orchard. The Okanogan River water enters Aeneas Lake off the point of land on the east shore. This pumping and irrigation program has been in operation for around 20 years and creates a high flushing rate, nutrient loss, and a degree of outside contamination. People who have fished at Aeneas Lake for many years claim the quality of fishing was better before the advent of the orchard irrigation and Okanogan River pumping.

Rainbow trout at Aeneas Lake, largely due to its scud population, are strong, healthy, and grow quickly. They are active fighters with the occasional "hot" fish that runs well into the backing. Typical trout are 12-16 inches with those elusive fish that exceed 20 inches. The north end receives the most fishing pressure; however, I have had excellent success along parts of the south end and west side. Aeneas Lake has been home for many years to pairs of highly skilled osprey. I have witnessed their expertise on several occasions as they picked off surface-cruising trout.

To reach Aeneas Lake from Highway 97 in Tonasket, turn west at the Loomis/Nighthawk recreation sign and drive 1/3 mile to a T-intersection (Loomis-Oroville Road). Turn left and head south for 1/2 mile to the Pine Creek Road and Aeneas Lake signs. Turn right on Pine Creek Road and head westerly for 3.6 miles to the public fishing access turnoff. Turn on the dirt access road and drive a short distance to the south shore of Aeneas Lake.

Sunrise at Aeneas Lake.

Dry Falls Lake

	106	107	108	109	110	111	112	113	114	115	116	117	118	119
90	91	92	93	94	95	96	97	98	99	100	101	102	103	104	105
74	75	76	77	78	79	80	81	82	83	84	85 ■	86	87	88	89
58	59	60	61	62	63	64	65	66	67	68	69	70	71	72	73
	58	44	45	46	47	48	49	50	51	52	53	54	55	56	57
	58	30	31	32	33	34	35	36	37	38	39	40	41	42	43
			22	23	24	25	26	27	28	29				

Washington Atlas &
Gazetteer Mapping
Grid

Dry Falls Lake is located in Grant County (T24N R28E S6), 3 miles west of Coulee City in Sun Lakes State Park. The lake is situated along the base of the westernmost cliffs of Dry Falls at the head of Lower Grand Coulee. (See *Washington Atlas and Gazetteer* pg. 85, D-6 and U.S.G.S. Coulee City.) [SPECIAL REGULATIONS]

At an altitude of 1,207 feet, Dry Falls Lake covers 99 surface acres with a maximum depth of 30 feet and mean depth of 10 feet. Dry Falls Lake is a waterfall plunge pool, its basin shaped by powerful forces of an enormous, ancient waterfall. The violent past evident here is very difficult even to imagine. The lake's setting is rugged and stunning, surrounded by 400-foot basalt cliffs with a large basalt island in the central part of the lake basin. The Dry Falls Interpretive Center and viewpoint sits on top of the canyon rim above the lake's southwest shore.

The shoreline is entirely covered with a heavy growth of reeds, especially along the southwest half of the lake. The southwest half is shallow, less than 5 feet in depth, with several small islands of reeds. A dense growth of submersed aquatic vegetation covers its entire bottom and hosts an abundant population of aquatic food sources—you name it. The northeast half of the lake has many areas with a steep bottom slope, dropping quickly down to 20-25 feet. Its entire littoral bottom is covered with weeds which, like the southwest half, are packed with aquatic trout food.

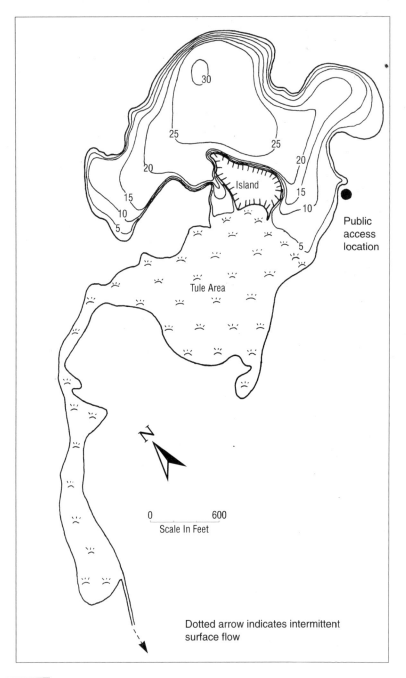

30

25

25

20

20

Island

15

15

10

10

5

5

Public access location

Tule Area

N

0 ———— 600
Scale In Feet

Dotted arrow indicates intermittent
surface flow

Dry Falls Lake and the westernmost cliffs of Dry Falls.

The lake is fed primarily by groundwater seepage and a low, 2-foot dam at the outlet (extreme southwest end) helps stabilize the lake.

Rainbow and brown trout in Dry Falls Lake are strong, healthy fish, popular with many anglers for their fighting abilities. They are quite adept at diving into weeds and slipping the hook. Most fish will be in the 12- to 18-inch range with larger fish to 20-plus inches. Despite the obvious hazards, some very nice, bold fish spend time cruising the weeds throughout the lake's shallow southwest half, even at mid-day. The Grand Coulee is a magnet for strong winds that seem to take special pleasure in blowing all anglers off the water—be prepared!

To reach Dry Falls Lake from U.S. 2 at Dry Falls Junction, turn south on Highway 17 toward Soap Lake and Ephrata. Drive 4.1 miles to the Sun Lakes State Park turnoff and enter the park. Drive 1 1/4 miles to a signed left-hand turn for Dry Falls Lake. From the left turn, head east then north, following the signs for 3 miles to the lake. The final mile-and-a-half is on a relatively rough and rutted dirt road that heads past Perch Lake to the south side of Dry Falls Lake. Walking around the lake and exploring the sage and basalt-covered land in the Grand Coulee basin is popular with many people; if you do this, be sure and keep a sharp lookout for rattlesnakes.

Grand Coulee and Dry Falls

The landscape of south and central eastern Washington is quite unique—an extensive lava plateau (Columbia Plateau) of basalt rock—a dense, black, crystalline lava, scarred by mazes of coulees, channels, and potholes (enormous, gaping hollows in the basalt). The most spectacular of these features is the Grand Coulee, a channel once occupied by the ancient Columbia River. Situated in the northwestern part of the Columbia Plateau, the Grand Coulee is a two-stage gorge about 50 miles long, covering 250 square miles. Its chiseled course, enclosed by impressive cliffs and desolate scablands, extends southwest from the Columbia River's present course, near the Grand Coulee Dam, all the way to the Quincy Basin north of Ephrata. It ranges from 1 to 6 miles wide and is lined by steep-walled cliffs up to 900 feet high.

The Grand Coulee is divided into upper and lower sections by a table of basalt, which underlies the region and covers more than 100,000 square miles in Washington, Oregon and Idaho. At the southern end of this table is a series of scalloped cliffs, twisting and turning their way for several miles across the Coulee. They form the foundation for what was once the largest waterfall in the world and are known today as Dry Falls—the remnant of an ancient waterfall that would dwarf present-day Niagara Falls. The meltwater-swollen Columbia River thundered over the basalt cliffs at Dry Falls creating an amazing spectacle about 3.5 miles wide and 400 feet high. Dry Falls began 20 miles to the southwest of its present location and receded upstream through the process of cataract retreat, leaving behind a gaping channel that today forms Lower Grand Coulee. This enormous 20-mile-long cut is one of the best examples of a receded waterfall gorge.

The following is a brief description of some of the theories that were proposed by geologist J. Harlen Bretz and defended for over four decades. His theories were finally accepted by the scientific community in 1971. By then he was over 80 years old. Catastrophism had virtually disappeared from geologic thinking over time as false ideas were accepted and the others unfortunately rejected. When Bretz presented his theories of massive, sudden changes to the earth's surface caused by tremendous flooding, geologists with a uniformitarian bias considered them in the same league as heresy of the worst kind. Today, more and more, sudden, catastrophic events are accepted as playing a significant part in the formation of many of earth's features.

As early as four thousand years ago massive lobes or fingers of the Cordilleran Ice Sheet advanced southward over northern parts of Washington, Idaho, and Montana blocking both Columbia River near what is now the Grand Coulee and Clark Fork River near the Idaho-Montana border. Vast glacial lakes (Lake Columbia and Lake Missoula), fed by meltwater and rainfall, backed up behind these enormous ice dams.

Lake Columbia, behind an ice dam of the Okanogan ice lobe, rose to an elevation of 2,400 feet—1,100 feet higher than present-day Franklin D. Roosevelt Lake

(Columbia River), the huge 151 mile-long, 81,000-acre reservoir created by Grand Coulee Dam. Eventually, water from Lake Columbia flooded over the north rim of the Waterville Plateau and was diverted down a structural depression in the basalt. This diversion of the meltwater-swollen Columbia River carved out much of the Grand Coulee.

Lake Missoula, behind an ice dam of the purcell ice lobe as much as 2,500 feet high across the Clark Fork Valley, rose to an elevation of 4,200 feet, contained 500 cubic miles of water with depths of up to 2,100 feet, covered 3,000 square miles (1,920,000 acres), and extended eastward for 200 miles, filling the interconnecting mountain valleys of western Montana's Rocky Mountains. In time, the lake became deep enough to leak out narrow paths in the top of the ice dam; these paths were enlarged by the water's erosive action, weakening the dam. Finally, the overwhelming pressure exerted by the lake on these weakened areas broke out enormous sections of the dam, sweeping it away. A wall of meltwater carrying huge icebergs raged south and west from northern Idaho into Washington and across the Columbia Plateau at depths of 200-800 feet (depending on the location) and speeds of 30-60 miles per hour—imagine the giant turbulence this created! Huge quantities of soil and rock were ripped from the earth and deposited in great hill-sized gravel bars along the flood's path all the way to the Pacific Ocean. Lake Missoula released up to 380 cubic miles of meltwater at an estimated maximum rate of over 9.5 cubic miles per hour. This is roughly equivalent to ten times the combined flow of all the rivers in the world! At this rate the lake could have drained in two days!

After this massive flood had spent its fury, the ice lobe continued to advance southward, forming another dam and lake—the ensuing flood further ravaging the land in its destructive path. This incredible process repeated itself until the ice retreated far to the north, the great ice dams fading into history. These Missoula cataclysms of virtually inconceivable power and magnitude repeatedly inundated nearly 16,000 square miles to depths of hundreds of feet. The Grand Coulee, shaped in part by previous Lake Columbia flows, was a natural course for some of these torrents, and was deepened and widened by merciless 200- to 300 foot-high walls of water and sediment that roared over and through the Coulee, carving their way to the sea.

Between periods of Lake Missoula's flooding, the mighty Columbia River, still diverted by the great ice dam, continued to flow down the Grand Coulee and thunder over massive falls. The awesome cataract at Dry Falls disappeared forever when the glaciers receded far enough north to reopen the Columbia's original channel. The river returned to its previous and present course leaving Grand Coulee high and dry. Dry Falls today is a quiet reminder of the massive, turbulent river that plunged over its precipice into the lower canyon of the Grand Coulee.

Now distinguished by extensive coulees, channels, and potholes, the Columbia Basin region tells the compelling story of massive flooding—and quite a story it is; very few places in the world can compare to the extraordinary scarring and erosion of south and central eastern Washington.

Today Grand Coulee, much like the rest of the Channeled Scablands, contains an array of "kolk" lakes—vestiges of the grinding force that shaped them. (Kolk is German for deep pool, scour, hole eroded by rushing water.) The Upper Grand Coulee, except for a few small seep lakes, was dry until 1951 when water was pumped from Franklin D. Roosevelt Lake to form 27,000-acre Banks Lake. Banks Lake is secured by North Dam and Dry Falls Dam, both earth-fill dams, that hem in the lake on both the north and south ends of Upper Grand Coulee. Each year water is pumped from Roosevelt Lake into Banks Lake where water is stored for irrigating over 500,000 acres of the Columbia Basin; land that was once unproductive desert is now fertile and grows abundant crops. Lower Grand Coulee, on the other hand, encompasses a scattering of smaller lakes and a chain of several large lakes that fill depressions scoured in the basalt by the violent water flows of ancient times. Many of these lakes are sustained by groundwater seepage and embody the main attraction of Sun Lakes State Park.

Perched on the northwest rim of the lower Coulee is the Dry Falls Interpretive Center which provides detailed information about Dry Falls and stunning views of both Dry Falls and Dry Falls Lake. Access is just off Highway 17 about 2 miles southwest of Dry Falls Junction, where Highway 17 joins U.S. 2.

(See Cataclysms on the Columbia, by Allen, Sargent, and Burns, and published by Timber Press of Portland, Oregon. This book contains detailed information about both the huge floods and geologist J. Harlen Bretz, who comprehensively studied the Columbia Basin region and proposed the now accepted theory that a massive series of floods were responsible for its unique features. To order this and other excellent resources, please contact the Northwest Interpretive Association at (206) 553-7958 or 83 South King Street, Suite 212; Seattle, WA 98104.)

Lenore Lake

Lenore Lake is located in Grant County (T23N R26E S 1, 11, 12, 14, 23, 26, 35), about 4.5 miles north of the city of Soap Lake. It is part of Sun Lakes State Park and Lake Lenore Wildlife Area in Lower Grand Coulee. (See *Washington Atlas and Gazetteer* pg. 68, A-4 and 84, D-4 and U.S.G.S. Little Soap Lake and Jameson Lake South East.) [SPECIAL REGULATIONS]

At an altitude of 1,074 feet, Lenore Lake is 5.5 miles long and covers 1,300 surface acres. Maximum depth is 27 feet with a mean depth of 15 feet. This depth is surprising considering the configura-

| 106 | 107 | 108 | 109 | 110 | 111 | 112 | 113 | 114 | 115 | 116 | 117 | 118 | 119 |

Washington Atlas &
Gazetteer Mapping
Grid

tion of the surrounding shoreline topography. Lenore Lake lies in the lower Grand Coulee where high basalt cliffs rise over 600 feet above both sides of the lake basin. These spectacular cliffs drop straight down into Lenore Lake along its entire west shoreline and in a few places along the east shoreline. The lake's bottom slope along these areas is very steep; however the cliffs do not extend as far down into the lake as one would expect. On the other hand, the bottom slope at the south end and along most of the east shoreline is gradual, resulting in extensive shallows. Gentle, grassy meadows border the lake along these areas. The littoral bottom is very rocky with scattered areas of submersed weed growth.

The lake is fed by surface runoff and intermittent flow from adjacent Alkali Lake; there is no surface outlet. Water level is controlled by pumping and has been monitored by the U.S. Geological Survey since 1938. The water in Lenore Lake is very mineralized and alkaline. Because of this, the lake for many years could not support fish life. This presented another opportunity for Lahontan cutthroat trout (introduced in the early 1980s) that now survive and thrive in the waters of Lenore Lake. They grow to impressive proportions and have created an outstanding fishery from a once barren lake. Lenore Lake was originally called Alkali Lake and included present-day Alkali Lake to the northeast. Alkali Lake was separated around 1930 by a small dam and a highway. Lenore Lake was renamed in 1932. There are a

Lenore Lake and Cliffs of Lower Grand Coulee.

   Washington's Best Lake Fly Fishing

few small bedrock islands and one large 14.5 acre island at the south half of the lake.

Lahontans average 16-22 inches with larger fish to 10 pounds. I have found good success early and late in relatively shallow water at the lake's south end and along the south half of the east shoreline. Heavy winds are common throughout the area and can spoil fishing very quickly. It does not take much of a wind to build up very large waves over the wide-open length of Lenore Lake.

To reach Lenore Lake from U.S. 2 at Dry Falls Junction, turn south on Highway 17 toward Soap Lake and Ephrata and drive about 12 miles to the north end of Lenore Lake. Public access areas are off the highway along the lake's east shore for the next several miles.

Washington Atlas & Gazetteer Mapping Grid

Jameson Lake

Jameson Lake is located in Douglas County (T25N R25E S 1,12 and T25N R26E S6), about 8 miles south of Mansfield and 16 miles west of Coulee City near the head of Moses Coulee. (See *Washington Atlas and Gazetteer* pg. 84, C-3 and U.S.G.S. Jameson Lake West and

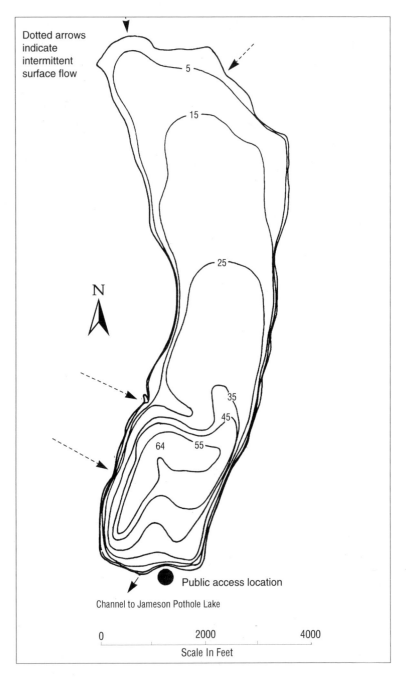

Dotted arrows indicate intermittent surface flow

5

15

N

25

35

45

64   55

Public access location

Channel to Jameson Pothole Lake

0   2000   4000

Scale In Feet

Jameson Lake East.) [SPECIAL REGULATIONS]

Jameson Lake covers 620 surface acres and lies at an altitude of 1,781 feet. Maximum depth is around 64 feet with a mean depth of 24 feet. Water level typically varies about 4 feet during the course of a year, altering depth and acreage slightly. Times of heavy rainfall have created runoff flooding in past years, significantly raising the water level. The lake is situated between the impressive basalt cliffs of Moses Coulee.

Jameson Lake is fed both by groundwater seepage and several small intermittent streams, one of which comes in at the north end from Bennett and Grimes lakes. Intermittent drainage is southward by overflow to Jameson Pothole Lake; at higher lake stages the two lakes merge to form a single water body. Reed growth covers about 1/3 of the shoreline area and the littoral bottom is mostly sand, silt, and gravel with local areas of submersed aquatic weed growth. A large percentage of this weed growth is at the north end which has extensive shallows and a gradual bottom slope. Irrigated farmland borders the north end of the lake. The south half of the lake has a steep bottom slope. There is a public boat launch and access point at the southeast corner of the lake, and a private launch and access point at Jameson Lake Resort at the lake's northeast corner.

Jameson Lake has been popular with anglers for many years and grows beautiful, strong rainbow trout—it is "home of the fighting rainbow." Rainbows average 10-16 inches with occasional larger fish to 20-plus inches. Due to standard harvest and equipment regulations, the lake receives heavy pressure from bait and hardware-trolling harvest anglers. Despite the heavy harvest, nice fish are still available and can offer excellent fishing. I have had my best luck fly fishing at the north half; access for the north end is by way of Jameson Lake Resort with a small fee for launching.

To reach Jameson Lake Resort on the lake's north end, turn from U.S. 2 onto north Highway 17 toward Bridgeport and drive 14.3 miles to Highway 172. Turn west on Highway 172 toward Mansfield and go 13.6 miles to Mansfield Road, following the sign for Jameson Lake at the east edge of Mansfield. Turn south on Mansfield Road and drive 9 1/4 miles to the lake.

To reach the public access and boat launch at the lake's south end, turn off U.S. 2 in Moses Coulee and head north on Jameson Lake Road. Drive 7 miles to the lake, passing through resort property next to Jameson Pothole Lake less than 1 mile before the public access area.

Grimes Lake

	106	107	108	109	110	111	112	113	114	115	116	117	118	119
90	91	92	93	94	95	96	97	98	99	100	101	102	103	104	105
74	75	76	77	78	79	80	81	82	83	84	85	86	87	88	89
58	59	60	61	62	63	64	65	66	67	68	69	70	71	72	73
	58	44	45	46	47	48	49	50	51	52	53	54	55	56	57
	58	30	31	32	33	34	35	36	37	38	39	40	41	42	43
			22	23	24	25	26	27	28	29				

Washington Atlas & Gazetteer Mapping Grid

Grimes Lake is located in Douglas County (T26N R26E S20,29), at the head of Moses Coulee about 5.5 miles south of Mansfield and 2 miles northeast of Jameson Lake. (See *Washington Atlas and Gazetteer* pg. 84, C-4 and U.S.G.S. Jameson Lake East.) [SPECIAL REGULATIONS]

Grimes Lake lies at an altitude of 1,831 feet and covers 180 surface acres. Maximum depth is 67 feet with a mean depth of 24 feet. Grimes Lake, like Jameson Lake, is situated between high basalt cliffs of Moses Coulee, creating a stark, rugged setting. The water is quite alkaline and has always been too much so to support fish life—enter the Lahontan cutthroat. Lahontan cutthroat were introduced about 10 years ago and thrive in Grimes Lake. They have created an outstanding

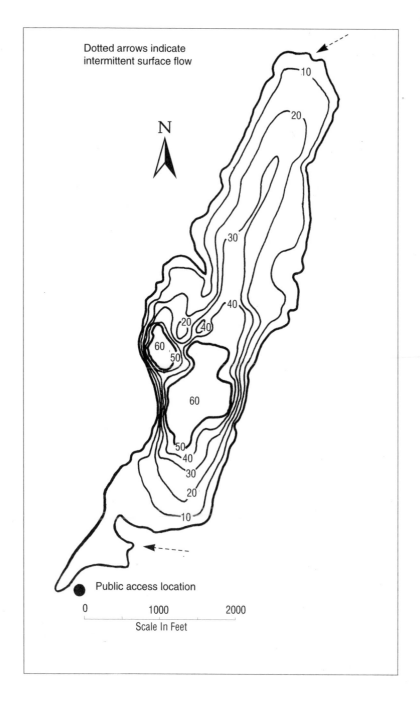

Dotted arrows indicate
intermittent surface flow

N

10
20
30
40
20
40
60
50
60
50
40
30
20
10

Public access location

0   1000   2000

Scale In Feet

fishery, once again, out of a barren, alkaline lake. Grimes Lake receives minor inflow from small intermittent streams at the north and south ends and drains southerly to Bennett Lake and eventually Jameson Lake. Reeds cover about 1/2 of the shoreline and submersed weed growth is relatively light.

Lahontan cutthroat in Grimes Lake are healthy fish and attain impressive proportions. They average 16-22 inches with larger fish to 8 pounds or better. The lake has abundant insect life, and appropriate imitations fished near the bottom in the shallower areas, especially early and late, work well.

Grimes Lake is surrounded by private land, and access is denied until fishing season opens. This is to prevent uncaring people from trashing and spoiling the land surrounding the lake. The season for Grimes Lake is very short, and opens just over 1 month later than the standard statewide opener. We are very fortunate to have a lake like this available for fishing, and it only takes a few uncaring people to spoil the fishing opportunities for everyone else. Please remember to leave the area cleaner than you found it.

Access for Grimes Lake is almost identical to that of north Jameson Lake. Turn off U.S. 2 onto north Highway 17 toward Bridgeport and drive 14.3 miles to Highway 172. Turn west on Highway 172 toward Mansfield and go 13.6 miles to Mansfield Road, following the sign for Jameson Lake at the east edge of Mansfield. Turn south on Mansfield Road and drive 8.1 miles to a signed gravel road for Grimes Lake on the left side of the road. Drive about 3/4 mile on the gravel access road (which is only open to public access during the season) to the south end of Grimes Lake. Watch out for rattlesnakes!

Nunnally Lake

Nunnally Lake is located on the 20,000-acre Crab Creek Wildlife Area in Grant County (T16N R23E S25,26,35,36 and T16N R24E S30), 8 miles southeast of Vantage and about 1.5 miles

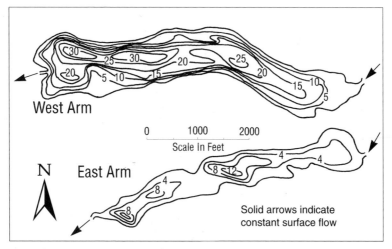

West Arm

East Arm

N

0   1000   2000
Scale In Feet

Solid arrows indicate
constant surface flow

east of the Columbia River. (See *Washington Atlas and Gazetteer* pg. 52, B-1 and B-2 and U.S.G.S. Beverly and Beverly South East.) [SPECIAL REGULATIONS]

   Nunnally Lake is about 2 1/4 miles long, lies at an elevation of 530 feet, and covers about 200 surface acres. Nunnally Lake is the westernmost and largest in a chain of 3 productive seep lakes. It was formed in the mid 1960s, along with Merry and Lenice lakes, by groundwater seepage. Columbia Basin irrigation projects (very possibly the Potholes Reservoir in the case of Nunnally Lake) forced water into underground cavities in the basalt lava rock which underlies the Columbia Basin region, creating many seepage lakes in the channeled

Basalt formation above the west arm of Nunnally Lake.

scablands. The Potholes Reservoir (first water storage in 1951) is about 26 miles northeast of Nunnally Lake.

Nunnally Lake has a west arm and an east arm (often referred to as Bobby Lake), divided by a very small, narrow channel. The west arm is the largest and deepest at 120 acres and 34 feet with a mean depth of 13 feet. Most of its littoral bottom is covered with submersed aquatic vegetation and nearly the entire shoreline is covered with reeds. The outlet area at the west end of the the west arm has been modified to stabilize the lake. The east arm is just under a mile long and covers about 80 acres. It is both narrower and shallower than the west arm with a maximum depth of 15 feet and mean depth of 6 feet. The littoral bottom is entirely covered with submersed aquatic vegetation that can choke large areas of the lake during the warm growing season. Shoreline areas are covered with a heavy growth of reeds. An inlet stream from Merry Lake flows into the east end of the east arm.

Nunnally Lake sits in the broken and rugged scabland country of central Washington where the wind can really pick up and blow! Its setting is one of desolation and rugged rock formations, the violent power of nature evident all around. Views to the south are dominated by the sheer, 2,300-foot upthrust ridge known as the Saddle Mountains, which are abruptly divided at Sentinel Gap by the Columbia River Gorge. Looking west from Nunnally Lake, the Saddle Mountains continue from the Columbia River Gorge as abruptly as they were divided. The lake itself is surrounded by basalt rock bluffs and extensive sand flats covered with sagebrush and broken by basalt outcroppings. The northwest corner of the west arm lies adjacent to a home, airstrip, and orchard. Game birds, predatory birds, and water-fowl are abundant in the area.

The lake is rich in nutrients, sustains abundant insect life, and very quickly grows large, healthy, well-conditioned trout known for their strong fighting qualities. I have had 15-inch rainbows bolt a few yards into my line backing and larger fish run nearly 40 yards into the backing! There are times when they hit like a freight train and times they act almost like a log. They also like to dive into the weeds after being hooked and can part light tippet like wet newspaper when doing this. I clearly remember an incident that occured once when I was fishing with an adult damsel dry fly. I hooked a strong fish whose weight felt like at least 6 pounds. After an animated struggle I finally worked the fish up to the surface and had a look at it—much to my surprise, I saw a large ball of weeds attached to the leader! I was lucky to land and release the 2.5-pound, 18-inch rainbow.

The rainbow and brown trout in Nunnally Lake average 14-18 inches with larger fish to 20-plus inches. Kamloops trout were stocked for several years during the 1970s to see if they would mature at 4-5 years of age (like they do in B.C.), enabling them to live longer and grow larger than the fish used throughout eastern Washington that mature at 2-3 years of age. (There is a high mortality rate after maturation.) The Kamloops were discontinued because the warmer water temperatures, among other factors, caused an early maturation and mortality at 2-3 years like the other rainbow trout. Nunnally Lake also has pumpkin seed sunfish which the brown trout feed on and help control. The lake was rehabilitated in 1988 to remove the popu-lation of sunfish and other non-trout species. The rehabilitation was not entirely successful due in part to the lake's feeder stream. During the rehabilitation some sunfish were able to escape to the feeder stream and also hide in the heavy marshy areas enabling them to survive.

To reach Nunnally Lake from Interstate 90 near Vantage, take the Highway 26/243 exit on the east side of the Columbia River Bridge and go south. After 1 mile turn off on the Highway 243 exit and head south toward Wanupum Dam and Beverly. Go 7.5 miles on Highway 243 and turn east on the Beverly/Crab Creek Road. To reach the west arm of Nunnally Lake, drive for 2 miles on Beverly/Crab Creek Road to the signed public fishing access on the left side of the road. Turn left and drive a short distance to the parking area. From the parking area, walk northerly for about 3/8 mile, following the trail across the sand and sagebrush flats. To reach the east arm (Bobby Lake) of Nunnally Lake, continue for another mile east past the west arm turnoff to the signed public fishing access on the left side of the road. From the parking area, walk northerly about 1/2 mile, following the trail through the Russian olive trees and across the sand and sagebrush flats. Watch out for rattlesnakes, ticks, and mosquitoes.

Merry Lake

Merry Lake is located to the east of Nunnally Lake in Grant County (T16N R24E S30,29), on the 20,000-acre Crab Creek Wildlife Area. It is 9 miles southeast of Vantage and 4 miles east of the Columbia River. (See *Washington Atlas and Gazetteer* pg. 52, B-2 and U.S.G.S. Beverly South East.) [SPECIAL REGULATIONS]

Merry Lake, about 540 feet above sea level, is a small water body covering about 15 surface acres. Maximum depth is 11 feet with a mean depth of about 5 feet. Merry is central and smallest in a chain of 3 productive seep lakes. It was formed in the mid 1960s, along with Nunnally and Lenice lakes, by groundwater seepage. It is situated in a relatively small gully and flanked on the north and south by steep

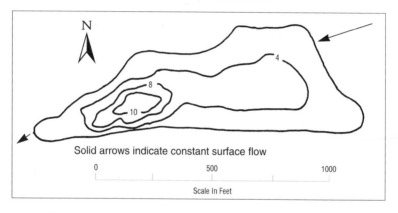

Solid arrows indicate constant surface flow

0   500   1000

Scale In Feet

basalt bluffs and outcroppings. Because of its location, Merry Lake receives some degree of shelter from the area's heavy winds. The wind does not create quite the havoc at Merry Lake that it does at adjacent Nunnally and Lenice lakes.

An inlet stream from Lenice Lake flows into the northeast end of Merry Lake, and an outlet stream flows from the west end a short distance to Nunnally Lake. The east half of Merry Lake is very shallow, averaging about 2-4 feet in depth. The lake is rich in both nutrients and organic sediment, and the entire lake bottom is covered with submersed aquatic vegetation that nearly chokes the lake during the warm summer growing season. A very heavy growth of reeds covers the shoreline and extends out into the lake in places, forming small islands and points. A fairly dense stand of Russian olive trees also surrounds the lake.

Merry Lake grows large, strong, and healthy rainbow and brown trout. They average 14-18 inches with larger fish to 20 inches. Because of the lake's physical size constraint, the fish do not make long runs quite like their counterparts in Nunnally Lake; however, their fighting qualities are excellent and they make every effort to rid themselves of the hook. Kamloops trout, like Nunnally and Lenice lakes, were stocked for several years during the 1970s. Merry Lake also has pumpkin seed sunfish which the brown trout feed on and help control. The lake was rehabilitated in 1988 to remove the population of sunfish and other non-trout species. The rehabilitation, however, was not entirely successful. During the rehabilitation some sunfish were able to escape to the feeder stream and also hide in the heavy marshy areas enabling them to survive.

To reach Merry Lake from Interstate 90 near Vantage, take the Highway 26/243 exit on the east side of the Columbia River Bridge and go south. After 1 mile turn off on the Highway 243 exit and head south toward Wanupum Dam and Beverly. Go 7.5 miles on Highway 243 and turn east on the Beverly/Crab Creek Road. Drive 4.2 miles (1.2 miles further east from Nunnally's east arm turnoff) to an unsigned turnoff at a junk pile on the left side of the road. From the parking area, walk northerly for about 3/4 mile, following the path across the sand and sagebrush flats, down into a gully and through the stand of Russian olive trees to the south east corner of the lake. The launching area is just a narrow opening in the reeds, and along with the lake's muck bottom, can create a bit of a challenge in launching. Watch out for rattlesnakes, ticks, and mosquitoes.

Lenice Lake

Lenice Lake is located to the east of Merry Lake in Grant County (T16N R24E S28,29,33), on the 20,000-acre Crab Creek Wildlife Area. It is 9.5 miles southeast of Vantage and 4.5 miles east of the

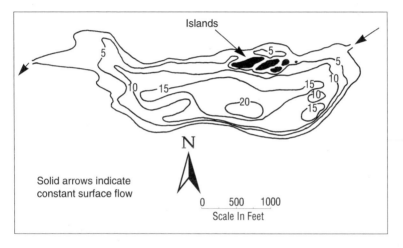

Islands

5

5

5

10 15

10

15

10

20

15

N

Solid arrows indicate constant surface flow

0   500   1000

Scale In Feet

Columbia River. (See *Washington Atlas and Gazetteer* pg. 52, B-2 and U.S.G.S. Beverly South East.) [SPECIAL REGULATIONS]

Lenice Lake lies at an altitude of 540 feet and covers 94 surface acres. It has a maximum depth of 23 feet and mean depth of 8 feet. Lenice is easternmost in a chain of 3 productive seep lakes. It was formed in the mid 1960s, along with Merry and Nunnally lakes, by groundwater seepage. The inlet area was modified to help stabilize the lake. Its setting, like that of Nunnally Lake, is dominated by views to the south of the Saddle Mountains. It is surrounded by basalt bluffs and outcroppings, sand flats covered with sagebrush and basalt rock, and stands of Russian olive trees. Like Nunnally Lake, the wind can

Looking along the Saddle Mountains from Lenice Lake.

really pick up and blow, making fishing very difficult at times. Of the 3 adjacent lakes (Nunnally, Merry, and Lenice), Lenice Lake is the most popular and receives the heaviest fishing pressure. This is primarily because it has the easiest access.

A partially spring-fed inlet stream flows into the northeast end of the lake, and an outlet stream flows from the small bay at the northwest end to Merry Lake. Nearly the entire littoral bottom is covered with submersed aquatic vegetation that supports an abundance of insect life. There is a sandy shelf along the southeast shoreline that is relatively free of weed growth; wave action prevents plant attachment along this unprotected area. The shelf is popular with anglers who like to wade and cast out over the dropoff, hoping to catch cruising fish near its edge. The northeast section of the lake has several bedrock and reed islands that provide another type of littoral structure. Fishing in-between and around them is popular with anglers, and produces many nice fish each year.

Lenice Lake grows beautiful, fat, and well-conditioned fish, popular for their fighting qualities. Like Nunnally Lake, these fish have "shoulders" to them and can really take line off the reel, not to mention diving into the weeds. The angler can expect most fish in the 14-to 18-inch range with larger fish up to 20 inches or more. Kamloops trout were stocked for several years during the 1970s to see if they would mature at 4-5 years of age (like they do in B.C.), enabling them to live longer and grow larger than the fish used throughout eastern Washington that mature at 2-3 years of age. (There is a high mortality rate after maturation.) The Kamloops were discontinued because the warmer water temperatures, among other factors, caused an early maturation and mortality at 2-3 years like the other rainbow trout. Like Nunnally and Merry lakes, Lenice Lake has pumpkin seed sunfish which the brown trout feed on and help control. The lake was rehabilitated in 1988 to remove the population of sunfish and other non-trout species. The rehabilitation, however, was not entirely successful. During the rehabilitation some sunfish were able to escape to the feeder stream and also hide in the heavy marshy areas enabling them to survive.

To reach Lenice from Interstate 90 near Vantage, take the Highway 26/243 exit on the east side of the Columbia River Bridge and go south. After 1 mile turn off on the Highway 243 exit and head south toward Wanupum Dam and Beverly. Go 7.5 miles on Highway 243 and turn east on the Beverly/Crab Creek Road. Drive for 5 miles to the signed public fishing access turnoff on the left side of the road. From the parking area, walk northerly about 1/4 mile to the lake.

Quail Lake

Quail Lake, at an altitude of 950 feet, is located in Adams County (T16N R29E S4), 5 miles north of Othello on the 23,000-acre Columbia National Wildlife Refuge. It is part of an area known as the channeled scablands. (See *Washington Atlas and Gazetteer* pg. 53, A-7 and U.S.G.S. Soda Lake.) [SPECIAL REGULATIONS]

	106	107	108	109	110	111	112	113	114	115	116	117	118	119
90	91	92	93	94	95	96	97	98	99	100	101	102	103	104	105
74	75	76	77	78	79	80	81	82	83	84	85	86	87	88	89
58	59	60	61	62	63	64	65	66	67	68	69	70	71	72	73
	58	44	45	46	47	48	49	50	51	52	53	54	55	56	57
	58	30	31	32	33	34	35	36	37	38	39	40	41	42	43
			22	23	24	25	26	27	28	29					

Washington Atlas & Gazetteer Mapping Grid

Quail Lake, originally called Clints Lake in 1951, covers 11.5 surface acres with a maximum depth of 36 feet and mean depth of about 15 feet. It is one of the O'Sullivan Seep Lakes, formed by groundwater seepage after the 19,000-foot-long O'Sullivan Dam was constructed from 1947-1949 to create the Potholes Reservoir. The Potholes Reservoir (first water storage in 1951) is 7 miles northwest of Quail Lake.

Quail Lake is a kolk lake (see section after Dry Falls Lake on Grand Coulee and Dry Falls), its basin carved from bedrock by powerful forces of water and sediment. There are no inlet or outlet streams—the lake is fed and drained by groundwater seepage. All but the southwest corner of Quail Lake is enclosed by short basalt bedrock walls and grassy, sagebrush-covered uplands. A small dike was added at the southeast corner of the lake several years back to raise and stabilize the water level. The southwest corner of Quail Lake is about 100 yards from the northeast corner of adjacent Herman Lake. Reeds cover the entire shoreline and choke the small bays on the lake's north end. The bottom slope along the central east and west shoreline is very steep, as the surrounding basalt rock walls would indicate. The littoral bottom is completely covered by a heavy growth of submersed aquatic vegetation that hosts many of the usual aquatic critters. The area is known for frequent winds and has abundant waterfowl, deer, game birds, cats, rabbits, etc. Watch out for rattlesnakes, mosquitoes, and ticks!

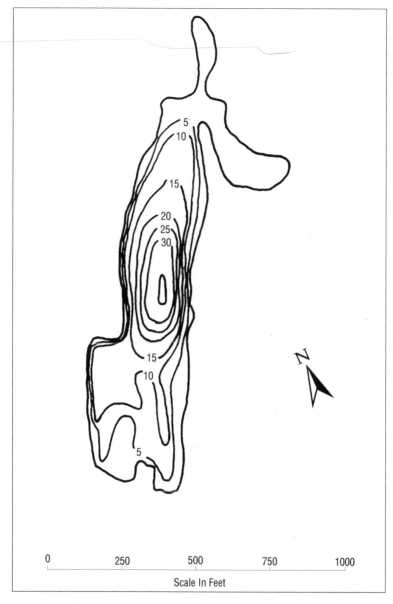

Quail Lake grows nice rainbow and brown trout that average 12-16 inches with larger fish to 20 inches. The lake was rehabilitated in 1991 to remove sunfish and other non-trout species. The rehabilita-

Looking southwest from Quail Lake to Herman Lake and the Saddle Mountains at sunrise.

tion was not entirely successful due to the lake's numerous groundwater seeps. During the rehabilitation period some sunfish were able to find these seeps, providing them enough oxygen to survive the rehabilitation.

Access for Quail Lake is from Highway 26 at Othello. Turn north off Highway 26 at the Othello turnoff (just opposite the west Highway 24 exit) onto the main road through town. It becomes 1st Avenue and goes north 1 1/4 miles to a T-intersection at Fir Street. Turn left on Fir for one block to Broadway Avenue. Turn right on Broadway, which becomes McManamon Road after leaving town and shifting to the northwest, and go 4.8 miles to the public fishing access sign for the "Seep Lakes." Turn right on the gravel road and drive 1.1 miles to a sign for Herman and Quail lakes. Branch off to the right and go a short distance to the parking area at the south end of Herman Lake. From the parking area, follow the Quail Lake trail in a northerly direction just over 1/4 mile to the south side of Quail Lake. The trail parallels the east side of Herman Lake and crosses a fence through a steel bar gateway to the lake.

Storm front approaching Wenas Lake.

Region 3

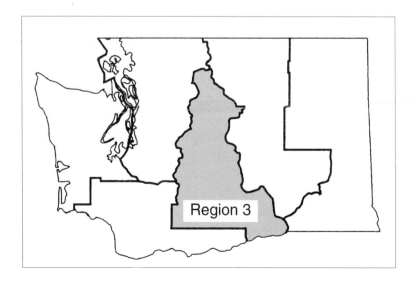

Region 3

Wenas Lake

	106	107	108	109	110	111	112	113	114	115	116	117	118	119
90	91	92	93	94	95	96	97	98	99	100	101	102	103	104	105
74	75	76	77	78	79	80	81	82	83	84	85	86	87	88	89
58	59	60	61	62	63	64	65	66	67	68	69	70	71	72	73
	53	44	45	46	47	48	49	50	51	52	53	54	55	56	57
	58	30	31	32	33	34	35	36	37	38	39	40	41	42	43
			22	23	24	25	26	27	28	29				

Washington Atlas & Gazetteer Mapping Grid

Wenas Lake is located in Yakima County (T15N R17E S2,3), 15 miles northwest of Yakima in the Wenas Valley. (See *Washington Atlas and Gazetteer* pg. 50, B-3 and U.S.G.S. Wenas Lake.) [SPECIAL REGULATIONS]

Wenas Lake lies at an altitude of 1,861 feet (at dam spillway) and covers about 75 surface acres at high water. Maximum depth at high water is about 40 feet with a mean depth of around 20 feet. The lake was created by a dam on Wenas Creek in 1946 and is managed by the Wenas Irrigation District for irrigation purposes. Acreage and depth can vary widely from nearly dry to about 75 acres. It lies in an agricultural valley surrounded by dry, rolling ridges covered with sparse grasses and sagebrush. The Wenas Lake Campground and Restaurant is at the north corner of the lake. Inflow is from Wenas Creek which flows into the lake's northwest corner. The littoral bottom is silty and because of the wide water level fluctuation, has very little in the way of submersed weed growth. Aquatic insect life is moderate.

Wenas Lake is known for large brown trout that feed almost exclusively on the lake's abundant population of shiners, allowing them to reach trophy-sized proportions. Wenas Lake gets pressure from bait and hardware-trolling anglers and has a fairly heavy fish

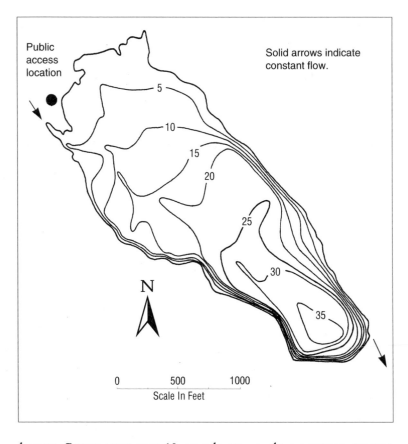

Public access location

Solid arrows indicate constant flow.

5

10

15

20

25

30

35

N

0   500   1000
Scale In Feet

harvest. Brown trout over 10 pounds are caught every year; average size is 12-16 inches. The lake also contains rainbow trout that are usually in the 8- to 14-inch range. Rainbows that feed primarily on shiners grow to 20-plus inches. Brown trout are notorious night feeders and move into shallower water during low light conditions to prey upon shiners or leeches. Best bet for fly anglers is to work the shallows early and late in the day with forage fish imitations or dark Woolly Bugger-type flies. For those of you who enjoy this type of fishing, Wenas Lake can provide an opportunity for a monster brown trout.

To reach Wenas Lake from Interstate 82 just north of Yakima, take the North Highway 823 exit for Selah. Follow North Highway 823 through Selah and out of town to North Wenas Road (Highway 823 becomes North Wenas Road after leaving town) which follows the Wenas Valley in a northwesterly direction to Wenas Lake. Drive 18.5 miles to the public access sign at the far northwest corner of Wenas Lake.

Wenas Road

From the town of Selah, Wenas Road follows the Wenas Valley in a northwesterly direction along the north side of Wenas Creek, and passes Wenas Lake. It continues to the head of Wenas Valley then turns north and climbs around the west end of Umtanum Ridge to a 3000-foot pine and aspen-covered plateau. From there it turns east and descends from Ellensburg Pass to twist and turn its way along Umtanum Creek, follow swelling ridges and narrow canyons, and finally reach the Kittitas Valley and the city of Ellensburg far below. I brought you along this isolated route, not so we can discuss the stark and irregular terrain it negotiates, but to share the history it represents.

During the 1870s wagons and stage coaches hurtled and jounced their passengers along this route, which was part of the long trek from The Dalles on the Columbia River to the settlement of Ellensburgh (proper spelling prior to the year 1894). The route was both practical and convenient as it connected growing areas of population and nicely threaded the geographic impasse provided by nature. During this time a settler named Jacob Durr operated a toll road that was shorter than the main route by 10 miles. Durr's road accomplished this by crossing over Umtanum Ridge east of the main route. He charged an annual toll of 25 dollars for this convenience. The word convenience, however, falls significantly short when it comes to an accurate description of Durr's road. The road was so nerve-racking that wagons had to use turntables to maneuver the switchbacks. According to one stage driver, Hell will not be a reality in the life to follow; it already exists between The Dalles and Ellensburgh.

Morning light on Rattlesnake Ledge above mist-covered Rattlesnake Lake.

Region 4

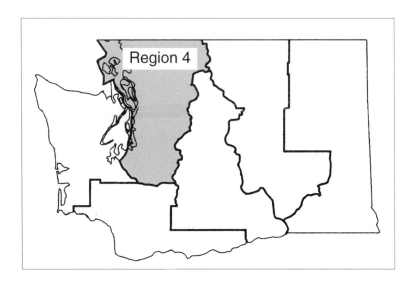

Pass Lake

		106	107	108	109	110	111	112	113	114	115	116	117	118	119
90	91	92	93	94	95	96	97	98	99	100	101	102	103	104	105
74	75	76	77	78	79	80	81	82	83	84	85	86	87	88	89
58	59	60	61	62	63	64	65	66	67	68	69	70	71	72	73
	53	44	45	46	47	48	49	50	51	52	53	54	55	56	57
	58	30	31	32	33	34	35	36	37	38	39	40	41	42	43
			22	23	24	25	26	27	28	29					

Washington Atlas & Gazetteer Mapping Grid

Pass Lake is located in Skagit County (T34N R1E S23), 3/4 mile north of Deception Pass on the south end of Fidalgo Island. The west end of the lake is in Deception Pass State Park. (See *Washington Atlas and Gazetteer* pg. 94, A-3. and U.S.G.S. Deception Pass.) [SPECIAL REGULATIONS]

At an altitude of 130 feet, Pass Lake covers 98 surface acres with a maximum depth of 25 feet and mean depth of 15 feet. It offers a nice, wooded setting in a beautiful island region views of 1,270-foot Mt. Erie which is 2.5 miles to the north; and some of western Washington's best fly fishing.

The water has an interesting and attractive greenish color with fairly limited visibility. This limited visibility and pea green color indicate a high concentration of plankton, and reflects the lake's ability to nourish and grow aquatic life. The nearshore lake bottom is mostly steep and rocky, descending quickly to depths of 10 and 15 feet. This partly explains the lake's lack of extensive weed growth areas. Weed beds at Pass Lake are located in areas along the lake's east end and around the point on the north side of the lake.

There are good populations of insects, fat-head minnows, leeches, and crayfish in Pass Lake, where one can expect to see a variety of water-

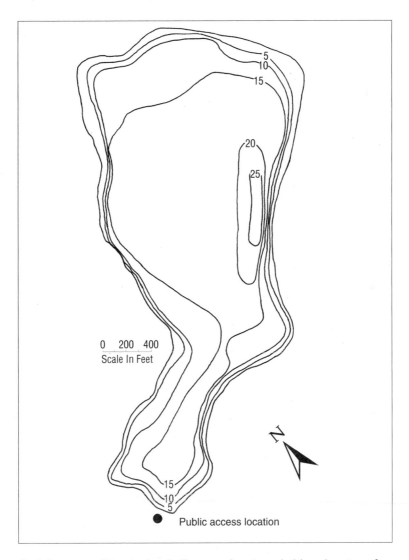

0   200   400
Scale In Feet

5
10
15

20

25

15
10
5

● Public access location

N

fowl, herons stalking in the shallows, and at times bald eagles. On a few occasions I have enjoyed spending the day with a pair of bald eagles. It was an added treat to watch them fly from perch to perch in the trees, then glide out above the lake waiting for a trout's final mistake. Twice I have observed an eagle dive out of its glide, skim the water, and fly off with a young trout that never learned.

Pass Lake and Mt. Erie.

Pass Lake is one of the most popular fly-fishing lakes in the state, receiving a great deal of angler pressure. This is because of its special regulations, proximity to a large population of fly anglers, and reputation for yielding large trout in a region where productive lakes managed for quality trout are few and far between.

Due to its year-round season and typically ice-free winter conditions, many fly anglers can be seen fishing Pass Lake during the winter. Fishing action, however, can get pretty slow as water temperatures are normally in the low 40s, considerably slowing the metabolism of the fish and causing them to become sluggish. Streamers are the pattern of choice during the colder months as trout feed on the lake's population of permanent organisms—fat-head minnows, crayfish, and leeches. Despite the cold, anglers have been rewarded with some very nice rainbows and browns.

Pass Lake was set aside in the early 1940s for special "fly-fishing-only" regulations. For a period of about 10 years (mid 50s to mid 60s) it was returned to general regulations. Several years later, fly fishermen began a successful movement to change the regulations back to fly-fishing-only and quality fish management.

Pass Lake contains rainbow, brown, and cutthroat trout and also some Atlantic salmon. The fly angler can expect most fish to be in the 12- to 18-inch range with larger fish to 20-plus inches available. Brown trout were introduced in 1989, and according to creel reports, are now the predominant catch along with rainbow trout. Cutthroat trout follow a distant third, and Atlantic salmon are seldom reported by anglers.

Lying adjacent to Highway 20, Pass Lake has excellent access. To get there from Interstate 5, turn west onto Highway 20, 4 miles north of Mt. Vernon, toward Anacortes/Whidbey Island. After 12 miles Highway 20 splits in two directions; the main branch turns 90 degrees south toward Whidbey Island and Pass Lake—the secondary branch continues west and north toward Anacortes. After turning south on the main branch, drive 6 miles to the lake. The parking and boat launch area is just off the highway at the lake's west end. Additional parking is available in spots along Highway 20, where it borders the lake's south side. Deception Pass Bridge is further along on Highway 20 about 3/4 mile south of the lake.

Deception Pass

Deception Pass, 3/4 mile south of Pass Lake, is a narrow, cliff-walled tidal strait, dividing Fidalgo Island (on the north) and Whidbey Island (on the south). Named "Deception Passage" by British naval officer Captain George Vancouver in 1792, it is known for a rapid current (to 8 knots) with boiling, churning whirlpools and eddies caused by tidal movement forcing large water volumes through the gap. Maximum depth in the gap is around 220 feet.

In June 1792 Joseph Whidbey, an officer in Vancouver's expedition, found the narrow strait. After Captain Vancouver was informed he realized that maybe his then-perceived peninsula was actually an island. Sure enough, the narrow strait divided the land and shaped what we know today as Whidbey Island. Before he found this passage, Captain Vancouver previously thought Whidbey Island was a peninsula—hence the name, "Deception Passage."

Ferry service across Deception Pass, catering to weekenders and vacationers, was offered beginning in 1913. This service was no longer needed when the impressive Highway 20 bridge came into existence. Its difficult construction in 1935 required two airborne leaps to get from Fidalgo Island to Whidbey Island. After crossing over very narrow Canoe Pass from Fidalgo Island, the bridge rests briefly on Pass Island before making its final stretch across Deception Pass to Whidbey Island. (Whidbey Island is the second largest island in the continental United States.) Each year millions of people stand on top of the Deception Pass Bridge (over 175 feet above the green, churning current) and admire the area's natural features from their birds-eye perspective. Turnoffs at either end of the bridge and on Pass Island allow visitors to park their vehicles and walk along the span.

Deception Pass State Park with picturesque scenery and diverse activities covers 3,000 forested acres both north and south of its focal point, Deception Pass. It offers 4 miles of shoreline, underwater scuba diving, swimming in two lakes, boating and boat rentals, picnicking, viewpoints, fresh and saltwater fishing, 251 campsites, facilities such as showers etc., and 27.5 miles of hiking trails including a 15-minute hike to 450-foot Goose Rock which offers views of the San Juan islands, Fidalgo Island, Victoria in British Columbia, and the 10,778-foot glacier-covered volcano, Mt. Baker.

Access to the main park (south entrance) is west off Hwy. 20, 0.6 mile south of the Deception Pass Bridge. Access to the Bowman Bay section of the park (north entrance) is west off Hwy. 20, 0.7 miles north of the Deception Pass Bridge. To contact the park, call (360) 675-2417, or write 5175 North Hwy. 20; Oak Harbor, Washington 98277.

Squalicum Lake

At an altitude of 477 feet, Squalicum Lake is located in Whatcom County (T38N R4E S7), 6.5 miles northeast of Bellingham. (See *Washington Atlas and Gazetteer* pg. 109, B-6. and U.S.G.S. Lawrence.) [SPECIAL REGULATIONS]

Squalicum Lake covers 33 surface acres with a maximum depth of 15 feet and a mean depth of 7 feet. The lake's extensive shallow areas provide excellent habitat for a heavy growth of submersed aquatic vegetation; which in turn supports a healthy population of midges, mayflies, caddisflies, scuds *(hyallela)*, damselflies, dragonflies, leeches, and snails. Reeds fringing the entire shoreline offer perfect emergence sites for some of these insects and give Squalicum Lake a "fishy" look and feel.

		106	107	108	109	110	111	112	113	114	115	116	117	118	119
90	91	92	93	94	95	96	97	98	99	100	101	102	103	104	105
74	75	76	77	78	79	80	81	82	83	84	85	86	87	88	89
58	59	60	61	62	63	64	65	66	67	68	69	70	71	72	73
	58	44	45	46	47	48	49	50	51	52	53	54	55	56	57
	58	30	31	32	33	34	35	36	37	38	39	40	41	42	43
			22	23	24	25	26	27	28	29					

Washington Atlas & Gazetteer Mapping Grid

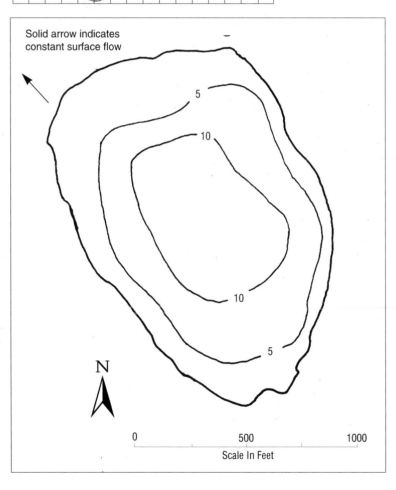

Solid arrow indicates constant surface flow

5

10

10

5

N

0   500   1000

Scale In Feet

Squalicum Lake is fed by underground seepage and drains westerly to form the headwaters of Squalicum Creek. The water has a high algal density and resulting limited water visibility. The lake is situated in a small bowl in the northeast shadow of 1,500-foot Squalicum Mountain, and is surrounded by gently sloping terrain of meadows and evergreen trees with grazing livestock and a few farm-like homes and outbuildings. Timbered foothills of the Cascade Range also rise to the east and south. These features combine to create a very attractive and peaceful rural setting.

Cutthroat trout are the main attraction for fly fishers at Squalicum Lake. They average 8-14 inches with occasional fish up to 20 inches. The lake sustains a natural spawning population of cutthroat and was last stocked in 1990. There have also been reports of small bass and perch, which hinder the trout fishery as they compete for available feed. It is important to remove these fish whenever possible.

To get there from Interstate 5, take east Highway 542 (Mt. Baker Highway) out of Bellingham and drive 6.3 miles from the I-5 interchange to the Squalicum Lake parking area; it is just off the south side of the road right before Highway 542 makes a 45-degree bend to the northeast. From the parking area, walk south about 1/4 mile to the lake—the route goes up a homeowner's driveway, around a gate and cattle guard, up a slight hill, and descends downward along a patch of evergreen trees to the lake.

Ebey Lake (Little Lake)

Ebey Lake, also called Little Lake, is located on top of 1,800-foot Ebey Hill in Snohomish County (T32N R6E S26), 6 miles northeast of Arlington. (See *Washington Atlas and Gazetteer* pg. 95, C-8 and 96, C-1 and U.S.G.S. Arlington East and Riley Lake.) [SPECIAL REGULATIONS]

Ebey Lake sits in a depression on Ebey Hill at an elevation of 1,509 feet and is known to have wide fluctuations in water level. At

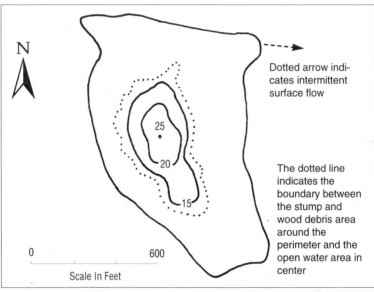

	106	107	108	109	110	111	112	113	114	115	116	117	118	119
90	91	92	93	94	95	96	97	98	99	100	101	102	103	104	105
74	75	76	77	78	79	80	81	82	83	84	85	86	87	88	89
58	59	60	61	62	63	64	65	66	67	68	69	70	71	72	73
	58	44	45	46	47	48	49	50	51	52	53	54	55	56	57
	58	30	31	32	33	34	35	36	37	38	39	40	41	42	43
				22	23	24	25	26	27	28	29				

Washington Atlas & Gazetteer Mapping Grid

N

25

20

15

Dotted arrow indicates intermittent surface flow

The dotted line indicates the boundary between the stump and wood debris area around the perimeter and the open water area in center

0   600

Scale In Feet

high water it covers 25 acres with a maximum depth of around 25 feet. This depth is surprising to many fly fishers who attempt to catch rainbow and cutthroat trout that inhabit the lake. The reason for their surprise lies in the deceptive nature of the lake basin structure. A fair-sized portion of its area, mostly the perimeter region, is occupied by large stumps, snags, beaver lodges, and submerged logs; while the central remainder of the lake is open water, free from these entanglements. The water depth around all the stumps, snags, and submerged logs is relatively shallow, leading one to believe that the adjoining open water area is shallower than a range of 15-25 feet.

The skeleton-like maze of stumps and snags, once an old growth forest logged around the turn of the century, creates quite a unique setting and adds an exciting challenge to the pleasant fishing experience available at Ebey Lake, which has been "fly-fishing-only" for over 20 years. Because of these stumps and submerged logs, many anglers find the fishing in and around them to be difficult, requiring both casting accuracy and an alert knowledge of the location and depth of the fly at all times. Even so, snag-ups occur and flies are lost even by the best of fly fishers.

Ebey Lake harbors a good population of some of the usual aquatic insects that include damselflies, dragonflies, mayflies, leeches, and snails. They provide nourishment for the pretty cutthroat and rainbow trout that normally range from 8-14 inches. Larger fish up to 20 inches are occasionally caught and will often be found lurking around the stumps and logs.

An alert observer has an excellent opportunity to see some of the wildlife that inhabit the area, including cougars. A fly fisherman one day at Ebey Lake told me about an encounter he had with a cougar. As he walked to the lake earlier that morning, he rounded a sharp turn in the path when there, less than 30 yards away, stood the cougar. Both man and animal were startled—the former frozen immovable and the latter bolting away at top speed.

Ebey Lake is surrounded by a fairly narrow greenbelt of trees that separate it from adjacent clear-cuts, one of which can be seen to the south of the lake. The lake contains very few submersed aquatic weeds and is fed by run-off water and groundwater seepage. It drains easterly to form Hell Creek which flows from the northeast corner of the lake, and after a few miles, spills into the North Fork Stillaguamish River. Hell Creek must have been named by anglers describing their experiences in attempting to find Ebey Lake for the first time. This difficulty lies in the multitude of logging roads which plaster Ebey Hill, the absence of any signs, and the fact that the lake cannot be seen from the road.

To reach Ebey Lake from Interstate 5, take the Highway 530 exit

(Arlington/Silvana) and head east. Highway 530 winds through Arlington and continues on toward Darrington. After 8.6 miles, just past Trafton, turn right onto Jim Creek Road. Jim Creek Road heads easterly, winding around the base of Ebey Hill. Drive 4.2 miles and turn left onto an unsigned gravel road (Ebey Mountain Road) that climbs up Ebey Hill. Make sure and stay on the main road as there are smaller roads branching off in places. At the 2.7 mile point the road crosses over Hell Creek; continue on for another 1.1 miles to the 3.8 mile point where a pathway access (on the left side of the road) to Ebey Lake begins. There are narrow places to pull off and park on the left side of the road. The pathway heads south and then west through the woods for about 250 yards to the northeast corner of the lake.

Note: the Washington state DNR has installed a gate (1995) across the Ebey Mountain Road at the 1.8 mile point from Jim Creek Road (2 miles short of the parking and pathway access spot for Ebey Lake). This closure is due to vandalism, garbage dumping, tree theft, and wildlife harassment by uncaring people. The future access and stocking status of Ebey Lake is uncertain at the time of this book printing. Please contact the Region 4 Department of Fish and Wildlife office for updated information on the situation.

Lone Lake

Lone Lake is located in Island County (T29N R3E S7), 5 miles northwest of Clinton on the south end of Whidbey Island. (See *Washington Atlas and Gazetteer* pg. 95, D-5 and U.S.G.S. Langley.)

At an altitude of 17 feet, Lone Lake covers 100 surface acres with a maximum depth of 17 feet and mean depth of 9 feet. The lake lies in a semi-agricultural area and is surrounded by timber, pasture, and several homes, the greatest concentration of which are situated along the east shore. Lone Lake has extensive shallows and a very gradual bottom slope. The entire lake bottom is covered with a heavy growth

	106	107	108	109	110	111	112	113	114	115	116	117	118	119
90	91	92	93	94	95	96	97	98	99	100	101	102	103	104	105
74	75	76	77	78	79	80	81	82	83	84	85	86	87	88	89
58	59	60	61	62	63	64	65	66	67	68	69	70	71	72	73
	58	44	45	46	47	48	49	50	51	52	53	54	55	56	57
	58	30	31	32	33	34	35	36	37	38	39	40	41	42	43
			22	23	24	25	26	27	28	29

Washington Atlas & Gazetteer Mapping Grid

of submersed aquatic vegetation which provides habitat for an abundance of aquatic food sources that include damselflies, dragonflies, leeches, mayflies, scuds *(hyallela)*, snails, and midges. The weeds grow tall in many areas of the lake and can limit the available fishing depth. Reed growth covers a large portion of the shoreline. Two small, intermittent inlet streams feed the lake, one flows into the northwest corner and the other into the northeast corner. An intermittent outlet stream drains from the southwest section of the lake. The water has a high algal density, supports a large population of zooplankton, and has limited visibility.

Lone is a rich lake that quickly grows fat, healthy, and active-fighting rainbow trout. An angler can expect most fish around 10-15 inches with larger trout to 20 inches. Lone Lake, because of its standard regulations, receives a heavy fish harvest from bait and hardware-trolling harvest anglers. With special regulations limiting fish harvest, prohibiting bait, and promoting catch and release, Lone Lake would contain a higher number of holdovers in the 16- to 20-inch range. The lake warms up quickly in spring and stays fairly warm throughout the summer. Because of this, the best fishing will be found early and late in the year.

To reach Lone Lake from Highway 525, 6.2 miles northwest of the Clinton Ferry and about 15 miles southeast of Highway 20, turn north

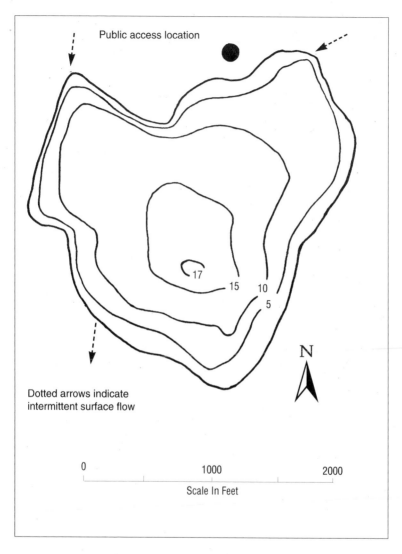

Public access location

Dotted arrows indicate
intermittent surface flow

N

17
15 10
5

0   1000   2000
Scale In Feet

onto Bayview Road. Drive north on Bayview Road for 1.8 miles and then turn west on Andreason Road. Head west for .6 mile and turn south (at the 90-degree turn where Andreason Road becomes Lone Lake Road) on the gravel access road for Lone Lake. Go south on the gravel access road for 1/2 mile to the parking and boat launch area at the lake's north shore.

Rattlesnake Lake

	106	107	108	109	110	111	112	113	114	115	116	117	118	119
90	91	92	93	94	95	96	97	98	99	100	101	102	103	104	105
74	75	76	77	78	79	80	81	82	83	84	85	86	87	88	89
58	59	60	61	62	63	64	65	66	67	68	69	70	71	72	73
	58	44	45	46	47	48	49	50	51	52	53	54	55	56	57
	58	30	31	32	33	34	35	36	37	38	39	40	41	42	43
			22	23	24	25	26	27	28	29					

Washington Atlas & Gazetteer Mapping Grid

Rattlesnake Lake is located 4 miles south of North Bend in King County (T23N R8E S34). (See *Washington Atlas and Gazetteer* pg. 64, A-2 and U.S.G.S. North Bend.) [SPECIAL REGULATIONS]

Rattlesnake Lake lies at an elevation of 911 feet and is known to have very wide fluctuations in water level—up to 25 feet! The lake covers 120 acres at high water level with a maximum depth of 54 feet and mean depth of 22 feet. The water level is at its highest in spring, lowering steadily throughout the summer months to reach a low point in fall. It has a striking setting, nearly surrounded by mountain ridges. The most prominent is Rattlesnake Ledge on the south end of Rattlesnake Mountain, rising over 1,000 feet straight above the west side of the lake. (A trail to Rattlesnake Ledge begins at the north end of the lake.) There are also good views of 1,655-foot Cedar Hill to the southeast and the ever-popular 4,167-foot Mount Si, 5 miles to the north, which rises about 3,600 feet above the city of North Bend. Mount Si (short for Josiah) is named after pioneer Josiah Merritt, who lived alone at the base of the mountain in a small cabin.

Rattlesnake Lake is commonly known as the water supply for North Bend—many also believe it is a water supply for the city of Seattle. This popular notion, however, is false. It is not a water supply for any city—unless they come and gather their water with buckets!

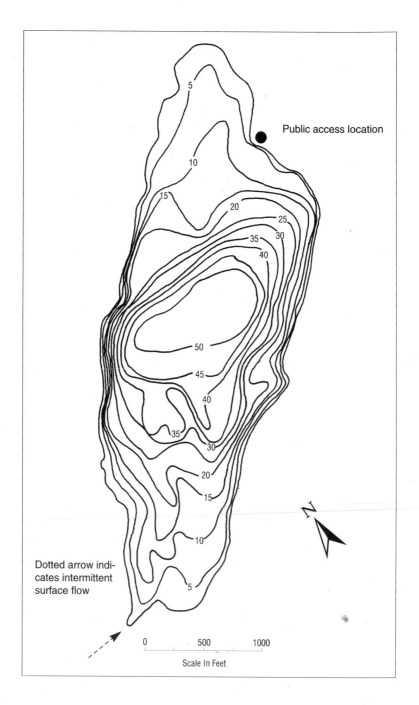

Public access location

Dotted arrow indicates intermittent surface flow

0   500   1000

Scale In Feet

(Rattlesnake Lake is not hooked up to any kind of piping system.) Before 1914 a portion of the present lake area was a marsh which became a small lake, known then as Rainy Day Lake, during years of heavy rainfall. From 1912 to 1914 a dam was constructed to create Chester Morse Lake (3 miles southeast of Rattlesnake Lake) which is a water supply for the city of Seattle. After Chester Morse Lake filled, groundwater seepage from a raised water table created Rattlesnake Lake. The wide water level fluctuations, for which Rattlesnake Lake is known, is due to the water level of Chester Morse Lake rising and falling, affecting the water table. I guess you could say, as Chester Morse Lake goes, so goes Rattlesnake Lake.

The lake bottom is rocky and relatively free of organic sediment with stumps scattered throughout. The lake is fed by groundwater seepage and a small inlet stream that flows off Rattlesnake Mountain into the southwest corner of the lake. Drainage takes place through underground seepage. The water is clear and relatively infertile with visibility up to 25 feet. Rainbow trout are stocked each year and are in good condition with a moderate amount of aquatic life to feed on, including forage fish. The rainbows average 8-14 inches with larger fish available, especially during years when brood trout are stocked.

Access is from Interstate 90 just east of North Bend. Take the 436th Ave. S.E. exit (number 32) and head south on 436th Ave. S.E., which shortly becomes Cedar Falls Road S.E. After 3 miles the road comes to the north end of Rattlesnake Lake where parking and boat launching is available. There is also additional parking just off the road along the lake's east side for nearly 3/4 of a mile.

Mount St. Helens looms to the southeast from Coldwater Lake.

Region 5

Coldwater Lake

	106	107	108	109	110	111	112	113	114	115	116	117	118	119
90	91	92	93	94	95	96	97	98	99	100	101	102	103	104	105
74	75	76	77	78	79	80	81	82	83	84	85	86	87	88	89
58	59	60	61	62	63	64	65	66	67	68	69	70	71	72	73
	58	44	45	46	47	48	49	50	51	52	53	54	55	56	57
	58	30	31	32	33	34	35	36	37	38	39	40	41	42	43
			22	23	24	25	26	27	28	29					

Washington Atlas &
Gazetteer Mapping
Grid

oldwater Lake is located in both Cowlitz and Skamania counties (T9N R4E S1,2 and T10N R4E S36 and T10N R5E S3o, 31),
31 miles east of Castle Rock and 7.5 miles northwest of Mount Saint
Helens' 8,363-foot summit. Coldwater Lake is located within the
115,000-acre Mount Saint Helens National Volcanic Monument. (See
Washington Atlas and Gazetteer pg. 33, B-6 and U.S.G.S. Elk Rock
and Spirit Lake West.) [SPECIAL REGULATIONS]

Coldwater Lake is about 3 miles long, 1/2 mile wide, covers 766
surface acres, and lies at an altitude of 2,470 feet. Maximum depth is
203 feet with a mean depth of 88 feet. It is situated in an awesome setting! The most stunning setting of any lake described in this book, as it
lies in the heart of Mount Saint Helens' blast zone. Views toward the
southeast are dominated by the only active volcano in the United
States. 5,610-foot Minnie Peak rises directly upward from the northeast end of Coldwater Lake, and 5,727-foot Coldwater Peak looks far
down from its perch above the lake's east side. Compared to pre-
eruption features, the surrounding topography looks foreign. (Mt. St.
Helens erupted Sunday, May 18, 1980 at 8:32 a.m.) What were once
heavily timbered slopes are now covered with volcanic debris and
skeleton-like tree remains. What were once lush stream valleys now

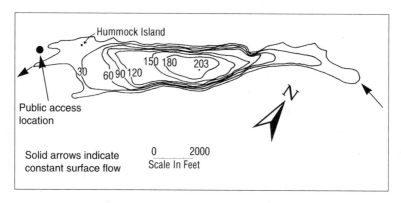

Hummock Island

150 180 203

30 60 90 120

Public access
location

Solid arrows indicate
constant surface flow

0 _____ 2000
Scale In Feet

N

are either filled with lakes or resemble the moon. What was once a
gorgeous, glacier-covered mountain now looms as a violent weapon of
destruction. Young vegetation, however, is making a slow comeback
on the surrounding slopes. The immensity and proportions of the
entire eruption and destruction that it caused is impossible to imagine. It is imperative to visit the area and see things first-hand.

Coldwater Lake was formed as a result of the May 18, 1980 eruption. The canyon in which the lake sits was once the home of
Coldwater Creek. The avalanche of volcanic debris that roared down
from the volcano settled in the valleys to the north of the mountain,
blocking the paths of several streams, including Coldwater Creek.
Water backed up behind this huge volcanic dam and began to fill up
the canyon. As the water began to reach the top of the dam, great concern for the probability of a catastrophic outbreak flood was voiced
and acted upon. The hope was to prevent water from cutting channels
across the loose rock and ash that blocked the valley and blowing out
the dammed area to flood the communities downstream. In 1981, the
Army Corps of Engineers used bulldozers and explosives to move tons
of earth and build a channel that would relieve pressure on the dam,
stabilize the lake, and allow water to drain from the lake in a gradual
manner. This work was also done to preserve the lake itself, as a
blowout would have destroyed the natural volcanic debris dam.

As the surrounding slopes would indicate, Coldwater Lake has a
very steep bottom slope. Coldwater Creek flows into the northeast end

Hummock Island and Coldwater Lake.

of the lake and drains from the southwest end to eventually meet the Toutle River. Aquatic vegetation is limited in areas of growth. This has mostly to do with the steep bottom slope, heavy winds that blow out of the northeast, and rocky nearshore lake bottom. Where given a chance, however, weed growth seems to be fairly abundant. Areas of weed growth include shallow, protected areas along the southwest end of the lake, along the westerly shoreline (particularly in the cove to the north of tiny Hummock Island), and along the northeast end of the lake. Aquatic food sources are relatively abundant with dam-selflies, dragonflies, caddiflies, mayflies, midges, and leeches. Overall aquatic life is good considering the lake has only been in existence since 1981.

Coldwater Lake contains beautiful rainbow trout that exist as a result of natural spawning. The lake was last stocked in 1989. Most fish will be 8-18 inches with occasional larger trout to 20-plus inches. The southwest half of the lake receives the greatest fishing pressure. However, the northeast end of the lake can provide outstanding fishing and a bit more seclusion. A boat with good oars or an electric motor is necessary to reach the northeast end, especially when the northeast wind comes down the canyon. Many anglers like to reach the northeast end before the wind blows and then ride it back to the boat launch.

Coldwater Lake has a parking area, boat launch, interpretive walkway, and outstanding facilities at the southwest end. A trail runs the length of the lake's westerly shoreline and is popular with many visitors. There are two fishing access spots off this trail, one about mid-lake and the other toward the northeast end. Staying on all the trails and walkways is imperative since a 100-dollar minimum fine is enforced for violators. This penalty has been instituted to protect vegetation and allow it to grow back. The Coldwater Ridge Visitors Center, perched on the canyon rim above the lake's southwest corner, has a gift shop, restaurant, and provides excellent information about the area and eruption. The Elk Bench trail descends from the visitors center to join the shoreline trail.

To reach Coldwater Lake from Interstate 5 at Castle Rock, head east on Highway 504 toward Toutle. Drive for 46.5 miles to the lake's parking and boat launch area. It is important to follow the sign for Coldwater Lake at the sharp left turn just before the visitors center.

(Please contact the Mount Saint Helens National Volcanic Monument for recreational information at (360) 750-3952 or 42218 N.E. Yale Bridge Road; Amboy, WA 98601. To receive a brochure for some outstanding resources (books, videos, etc.) that can be ordered and are worth every bit they cost, please write to Mount Saint Helens Visitors Center; Attention Northwest Interpretive Assoc.; 3029 Spirit Lake Highway; Castle Rock, WA 98611.)

Merrill Lake

Merrill Lake is located in Cowlitz County (T7N R4E S8,9,16,17,21), 27 miles east of Kelso and 9 miles southwest of Mount Saint Helens' 8,363-foot summit. (See *Washington*

	106	107	108	109	110	111	112	113	114	115	116	117	118	119
90	91	92	93	94	95	96	97	98	99	100	101	102	103	104	105
74	75	76	77	78	79	80	81	82	83	84	85	86	87	88	89
58	59	60	61	62	63	64	65	66	67	68	69	70	71	72	73
	58	44	45	46	47	48	49	50	51	52	53	54	55	56	57
	58	30	31	32	33	34	35	36	37	38	39	40	41	42	43
				22	23	24	25	26	27	28	29				

Washington Atlas & Gazetteer Mapping Grid

Atlas and Gazetteer pg. 33, D-6 and U.S.G.S. Cougar.) [SPECIAL REGULATIONS]

Merrill Lake lies at an altitude of 1,541 feet and covers 490 surface acres at high water level. Maximum depth at high water is 77 feet with a mean depth of 39 feet. The setting is attractive with a backdrop of mountain ridges covered with relatively young evergreen timber. The lake is situated in the heart of logging country—the surrounding ridges have been clear-cut more than once. The area bordering the shoreline has a greenbelt of older timber that has escaped the saw due to environmental purposes. Severe rainstorms in late January 1972 caused slides carrying mud, logs, and debris into the lake from the logged slopes. There is a good chance of observing wildlife such as elk, deer, and osprey. A couple pairs of osprey have nests in plain view at the tops of larger trees along the shoreline.

Merrill Lake has a very steep bottom slope. The north and south ends have the most gradual slope. The water level is subject to wide seasonal fluctuations. For example, during 1971, the observed lake stage varied 33.8 feet. Drainage takes place through underground seepage as there is no visible surface outlet. Inflow is from 3 main tributary streams as well as from smaller intermittent streams. 2 small islands exist in the north half of the lake. Weed growth is very limited due mostly to the wide water fluctuations and steep bottom slope. There are quite a few submerged tree stumps and snags along the

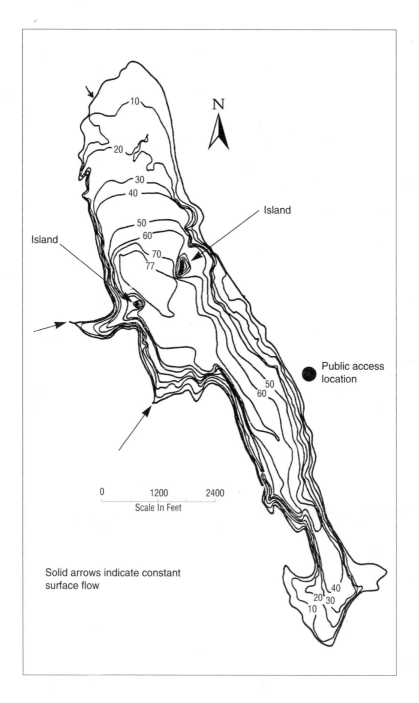

N

Island

Island

Public access
location

10
20
30
40
50
60
70
77

50
60

0   1200   2400
Scale In Feet

Solid arrows indicate constant
surface flow

40
20 30
10

nearshore lake bottom, especially at higher water levels. The fish seem to be attracted to these areas of structure.

Brown trout are stocked each year and average 10-16 inches with larger fish to 20-plus inches. Rainbow and cutthroat trout have also been stocked in past years. Any rainbow or cutthroat trout in the lake at present exist because of natural spawning. Brown trout are stocked exclusively because they are very resistant to a parasitic worm in the lake.

Despite relatively infertile water, Merrill Lake has a decent population of insect life that includes caddisflies, mayflies, midges, damselflies, dragonflies, and leeches. The insect of special note is the big yellow mayfly *(Hexagenia)* which is the giant among mayflies. The duns are over an inch long and should be imitated with size 6 and 8 hooks. They hatch in the northwest section of Merrill Lake from late afternoon until dark, mid-July to September. Spinners from hatches of the previous day or two return to the water just after the duns come off, making the whole thing seem like one big gathering. The fishing action that these insects provide can, at times, border on that of fantasy. If you see a hatch of these insects come off, do not be surprised if you think you are seeing birds. Also, keep in the back of your mind the fact that bats like these insects too. I talked to a couple of anglers once who swore their artificial flies sprouted wings and flew away!

To reach Merrill Lake from Interstate 5 at Woodland, head east on Highway 503 toward Cougar. Drive for about 28 miles on Highway 503 to the sign for Merrill Lake, less than a mile before Cougar. Turn north on Forest Service Road 81 and drive 4.8 miles to a signed (Natural Resources Recreation Site) dirt road that branches left and descends to the Merrill Lake campground, parking area, and boat launch on the east shore.

Anderson Lake.

Region 6

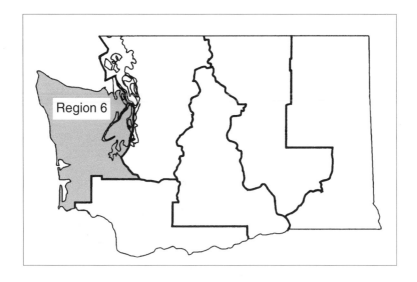

Anderson Lake

	106	107	108	109	110	111	112	113	114	115	116	117	118	119
90	91	92	93	94	95	96	97	98	99	100	101	102	103	104	105
74	75	76	77	78	79	80	81	82	83	84	85	86	87	88	89
58	59	60	61	62	63	64	65	66	67	68	69	70	71	72	73
	58	44	45	46	47	48	49	50	51	52	53	54	55	56	57
	58	30	31	32	33	34	35	36	37	38	39	40	41	42	43
			22	23	24	25	26	27	28	29					

Washington Atlas & Gazetteer Mapping Grid

Anderson Lake is located in Jefferson County (T29N R1W S9), seven miles south of Port Townsend on the Quimper Peninsula. Anderson Lake is the primary attraction of Anderson Lake State Park. (See *Washington Atlas and Gazetteer* pg. 94, D-2 and U.S.G.S. Port Townsend South.) [SPECIAL REGULATIONS]

Anderson Lake lies 250 feet above sea level, has an attractive setting, and covers 66 surface acres. It reaches a maximum depth of 29 feet with a mean depth of 19 feet. The nearshore lake bottom, with exception of the gradually sloping south end, descends quickly to depths of 20 and 25 feet. The littoral bottom at the lake's south half has an extensive growth of submersed aquatic weeds. Most of the shoreline is covered by reeds and lily pads, especially along the south end of the lake which is surrounded by a grassy meadow. Tree snags, floating logs, and other wood debris cover the shoreline in places, especially along the north half of the lake which is surrounded by heavy timber. The only nearshore development is the state park caretaker's residence along the west shore.

Anderson Lake and the adjoining land was privately owned for many years and used to raise cattle. The land was progressively acquired by the state from 1966-1969 and made into a state park. The

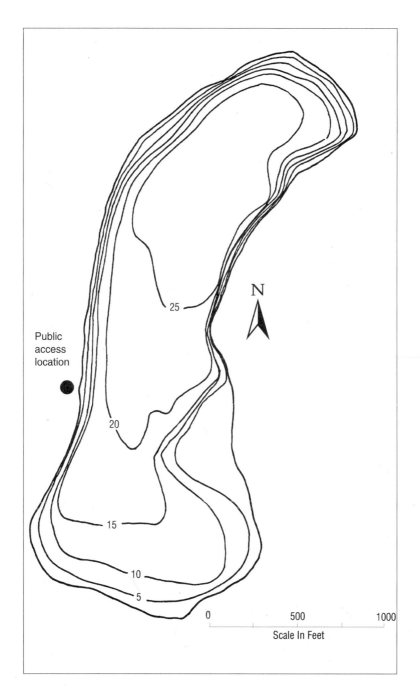

Public
access
location

N

25

20

15

10

5

| 0 | | 500 | | 1000 |

Scale In Feet

park is managed for day use only (no overnight camping), and has a boat launch area and hiking trails. There is now a fee for use of the boat launch.

Anderson Lake sustained a problem of low summer dissolved oxygen levels for many years, resulting in frequent summer fish kills. In order to eliminate this problem, an aeration system, completed in 1982, was installed to raise dissolved oxygen levels. The low summer dissolved oxygen levels were caused by a combination of warm water temperatures, thermal stratification, high algal density, and bacterial decomposition of organic matter. Bacteria use up available oxygen as they consume the different types of organic matter.

Anderson Lake is fed and drained primarily by underground seepage. The water has an excellent nutrient concentration and supports abundant insect life. Anyone who prowls the shallows in spring can see snails, cased caddis larvae, and damsel nymphs moving about, and find dragonfly and mayfly nymphs hiding in the weeds along with small *hyallela* scuds. This aquatic fauna supports active, healthy rainbow trout that average 10-14 inches. Larger fish up to 20 inches are also available. Eastern brook and cutthroat trout have also been stocked in Anderson Lake. The average fish size and number of large fish available are smaller than they could be because of the heavy fish harvest that takes place each year. This is due to part-year harvest regulations and the immense popularity of the lake with bait and hardware-trolling anglers. Despite this pressure, the lake produces some nice fish and can provide good trout fishing.

The angler who keeps an eye peeled for the many surrounding activities of nature will likely observe birds of prey in the process of survival, especially bald eagles and osprey. I once witnessed an osprey swipe a fish from the water and head for the trees. Within seconds a bald eagle streaked over the trees and dove for the osprey. With a lightning quick motion the eagle turned on its side and clipped the osprey, causing the bird to release its prize. Swiftly plunging to seize the fish in mid-air, the thief flew to a perch in the trees to consume its stolen meal. An impressive series of actions to say the least!

To reach Anderson Lake from U.S. 101, take north Highway 20 toward Port Townsend at the Discovery Bay junction. Drive 3.7 miles on Highway 20 (far above the east side of Discovery Bay) to Anderson Lake Road. Go east on Anderson Lake Road for 1.1 miles and turn north on the gravel state park access road. Drive 1/2 mile to the parking and boat launch area.

Discovery Bay

Discovery Bay, named in early May of 1792 by Captain George Vancouver, lies 1.5 miles west of Anderson Lake and projects inland 9 miles from its source, the Strait of Juan de Fuca. It ranges from 1-2 miles wide, and divides the mainland, forming the Miller and Quimper peninsulas. Captain George Vancouver arrived in northwest Washington state in spring of 1792. He and his men spent part of that summer carefully exploring and surveying the waters of the entire Puget Sound region. Many of the region's major features were named by Captain Vancouver.

It was here at Discovery Bay that Captain Vancouver and his men anchored ship to find and cut a new mast (spar) for his flagship, the Discovery. (The Discovery was a sloop, a fore-and-aft rigged, single-masted vessel.) Captain Vancouver sent his crew ashore where they completed this task. Apparently the task of choosing a mast was not particularly difficult, as Vancouver noted that the land offered "thousands of the finest spars the world produces." This is the first written mention of Washington state's exceptional forest resources.

Buck Lake

Buck Lake is located in Kitsap County (T28N R2E S21), on the north tip of the Kitsap Peninsula, 1/2 mile south of Hansville. Buck Lake County Park borders the lake's southeast shore. (See *Washington Atlas and Gazetteer* pg. 78, A-4 and U.S.G.S. Hansville.)

Buck Lake lies at an altitude of 140 feet and covers 22 surface acres. It reaches a maximum depth of 24 feet with a mean depth of 7 feet. Buck Lake is nearly surrounded by a heavy growth of trees and brush, and has a very "fishy" setting as there is abundant floating, submersed, and emersed (reeds) vegetation covering the shoreline. Aside

		106	107	108	109	110	111	112	113	114	115	116	117	118	119
90	91	92	93	94	95	96	97	98	99	100	101	102	103	104	105
74	75	76	77	78	79	80	81	82	83	84	85	86	87	88	89
58	59	60	61	62	63	64	65	66	67	68	69	70	71	72	73
	58	44	45	46	47	48	49	50	51	52	53	54	55	56	57
	58	30	31	32	33	34	35	36	37	38	39	40	41	42	43
			22	23	24	25	26	27	28	29					

Washington Atlas & Gazetteer Mapping Grid

from the small park at the southeast end of the lake, nearshore development is limited to a few homes back in the trees along the northeast shore.

Buck Lake is fed and drained primarily by groundwater seepage, and the water has a distinct amber hue caused by tannic acid from the decomposition of plant matters. Submersed aquatic vegetation covers the entire littoral bottom and is especially dense at the shallow north end of the lake. The shoreline is covered by a heavy growth of reeds; also, tree snags, floating logs, and other wood debris cover the shore in scattered areas. Lily pads cover the lake surface in a narrow margin close to shore, particularly at the north end of the lake. Beavers have also been at work, their design displayed on the southwest side of the lake.

Buck Lake has an excellent population of aquatic food sources and contains healthy, active rainbow trout averaging 10-14 inches with larger fish up to 20 inches. Eastern brook and cutthroat trout have been stocked in past years. Buck Lake has standard regulations and receives a heavy fish harvest. It is popular with bait and hardware-trolling harvest anglers. The lake would produce a larger fish on the average if it was given the opportunity. Some bass are also present which is not good for trout. There has been talk of rehabilitating the lake to remove the bass, but locals will have none of it. There has been a cooperative effort project to remove bass that are caught and

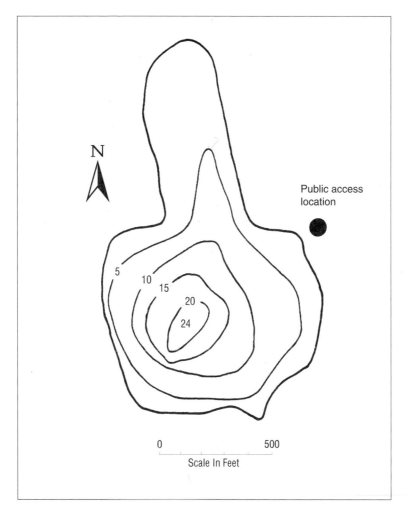

N

Public access location

5
10
15
20
24

0   500
Scale In Feet

transport them to other lakes.

To reach Buck Lake from Highway 104, 2.5 miles west of the Kingston Ferry, turn north onto Hansville Road at the stoplight intersection. Drive on Hansville Road for 7.4 miles to Buck Lake Road. Head west for 3/4 mile then turn off the road to the right at the signed public fishing turnoff a short distance before reaching the Buck Lake County Park entrance. A gravel road continues a short distance to the public access and boat launch area on the lake's northeast shore.

Morning at Buck Lake.

Hansville, 1/2 mile north of Buck Lake, is named after Hans Zachariasen, one of the early Norwegian settlers in the area. The site which later became Hansville was first settled in 1893 by a Norwegian herring fisherman and his partner who sold their catch to halibut boats in the area. Other Norwegians, including Hans Zachariasen, soon followed and started a community that exists to this day.

Prices Lake

Prices Lake, also called Price Lake, is located in Mason County (T23N R4W S22, 23), 4.5 miles northwest of Hoodsport and 2 miles east of Lake Cushman State Park. (See *Washington Atlas and Gazetteer* pg. 61, A-7 and U.S.G.S. Hoodsport.) [SPECIAL REGULATIONS]

Prices Lake covers 62 surface acres at an altitude of 780 feet. Maximum depth is 16 feet with a mean depth of 6 feet. The lake is situated in a basin surrounded by heavily timbered ridges and has a very

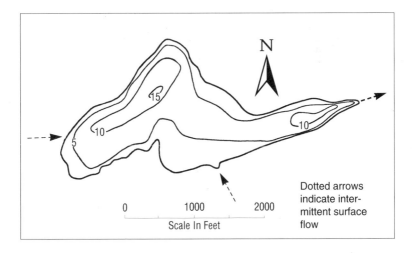

	106	107	108	109	110	111	112	113	114	115	116	117	118	119	
90	91	92	93	94	95	96	97	98	99	100	101	102	103	104	105
74	75	76	77	78	79	80	81	82	83	84	85	86	87	88	89
58	59	60	61	62	63	64	65	66	67	68	69	70	71	72	73
	58	44	45	46	47	48	49	50	51	52	53	54	55	56	57
	58	30	31	32	33	34	35	36	37	38	39	40	41	42	43
			22	23	24	25	26	27	28	29					

Washington Atlas & Gazetteer Mapping Grid

N

0   1000   2000

Scale In Feet

Dotted arrows indicate inter- mittent surface flow

tranquil, pristine setting. Views to the south are dominated by Dow Mountain which has a lookout on its 2,514-foot crest. 1,840-foot Saddle Mountain rises directly upward from the lake's north corner. There is no nearshore development.

Prices Lake has a very gradual bottom slope and extensive shallows. Submersed aquatic vegetation covers most of the lake bottom which is a very thick, silty muck. Submerged tree stumps that have snagged many artificial flies are scattered around the lake bottom. About 1/3 of the lake surface is covered by floating aquatic vegetation such as lily pads, etc. The shoreline is covered by reeds, brush, floating logs, tree snags, and other wood debris. Two intermittent streams

Prices Lake.

flow off Dow Mountain and into the lake; one at the west corner and the other mid-lake at the south side. Drainage is easterly to Lilliwaup Creek and the Hood Canal. According to reports, a resort once existed on the lake's south shore sometime around the 1940s. There are very few, if any, remains to verify its former existence. If one spends enough time searching they might find a few pilings from an old dock, maybe an old, sunken, wooden boat, or perhaps some rotten timbers from a building.

Rainbow, cutthroat, and brook trout live in Prices Lake and receive nourishment from a relative abundance of aquatic foods including damselflies, dragonflies, mayflies, caddisflies, leeches, and midges. The fish population is maintained partly by natural spawning and a wide range of age groups can be observed. Fish from 8 inches to 20 inches may be caught all in the same day. Prices Lake, similar to many lakes in the region, has a large population of salamanders or mud puppies. It is undetermined whether or not they hinder fish growth by competing for available feed. Prices Lake is best fished early in spring as the lake seems to warm quickly. Action can become quite slow during the late spring and summer months. Late fall can also be very good, however, access is difficult during this time as the dirt access road is closed to motor vehicles.

To reach Prices Lake from U.S. 101 at Hoodsport, turn west at the sign for the Cushman/Staircase Recreation Area and Highway 119 (Lake Cushman Road). Drive 8 miles (just over 1/2 mile past Lake Cushman State Park) and turn east on an unmarked dirt logging road. (This dirt logging road is closed to motor vehicles from October 1 to April 15 so as not to disturb the resident elk in their winter range.) Drive 2 miles, bearing to the left toward Saddle Mountain at the Y-intersection, to the parking area for Prices Lake. The parking area is just a small spot to pull off on the right hand side of the road. From the parking area, follow the access path downhill for about 200 yards through brush and timber to the northwest corner of the lake. The area for launching is just a narrow opening in the brush. This narrow entrance along with the lake's thick muck can make launching a bit of a challenge.

Appendix A
Stocking Data   (1989-1994)

WCT—Westslope Cutthroat
RB—Rainbow Trout, Resident
AG—Arctic Grayling

LCT—Lahontan Cutthroat
BT—Brown Trout
AT-Atlantic Salmon

CCT—Cutthroat, Coastal Resident
EB—Eastern Brook Trout

REGION 1

Lake	Date	Species	Avg. Size	Number	Pounds
Big Four	April/1989	RB	3 Pounds	506	1,792
Big Four	April/1989	RB	10 Inches	4,160	1600
Big Four	March/1990	RB	8 Pounds	50	400
Big Four	March/1990	RB	15.5 Inches	533	800
Big Four	March/1990	RB	10.5 Inches	3,960	1,800
Big Four	March/1991	RB	6.5 Pounds	13	87
Big Four	March/1991	RB	16 Inches	500	850
Big Four	Feb./1992	RB	11 Inches	3,052	1,795
Big Four	Feb./1992	RB	5 Pounds	27	135
Big Four	Feb./1992	RB	15.5 Inches	725	1,088
Big Four	March/1993	RB	11 Inches	3,458	1,820
Big Four	March/1993	RB	5 Pounds	30	150
Big Four	March/1993	RB	2 Pounds	300	600
Big Four	March/1994	RB	10.5 Inches	2,000	1,000
Big Four	March/1994	RB	14.5 Inches	656	853
Big Four	March/1994	RB	5.5 Pounds	30	165
Medical	March/1989	BT	7.5 Inches	5,071	805
Medical	March/1990	BT	7.5 Inches	5,005	910
Medical	May/1991	BT	9 Inches	2,940	840
Medical	April/1992	BT	8.5 Inches	5,000	1,250
Medical	April/1993	BT	7.5 Inches	5,016	880
Medical	March/1994	BT	8 Inches	4,002	870
Amber	May/1989	WCT	3.75 Inches	14,007	290
Amber	May/1989	RB	16 Inches	500	800
Amber	May/1989	RB	3.5 Inches	20,130	330
Amber	May/1990	RB	3.5 Inches	34,220	580
Amber	May/1991	WCT	4 Inches	10,125	225
Amber	May/1991	RB	3.5 Inches	24,115	455
Amber	April/1992	RB	3.5 Pounds	112	392
Amber	May/1992	RB	3.5 Inches	17,110	300
Amber	May/1993	WCT	3.25 Inches	5,070	65
Amber	May/1993	RB	5.75 Pounds	100	570
Amber	May/1993	RB	3.25 Inches	5,200	80
Amber	May/1994	RB	16 Inches	20	34
Amber	May/1994	RB	5.6 Pounds	80	448
Amber	May/1994	WCT	3.75 Inches	5,000	100
Browns	Sept./1989	WCT	2.25 Inches	8,000	32
Browns	Sept./1990	WCT	2.5 Inches	7,030	37
Browns	May/1992	WCT	5 Inches	3,520	160
Browns	May/1993	WCT	4.75 Inches	9,002	325
Browns	Oct./1993	WCT	2.5 Inches	15,041	84.5
Browns	Sept./1994	WCT	2.5 Inches	15,051	87
Nile	May/1989	EB	3 Inches	2,646	27
Nile	May/1991	EB	3 Inches	3,977	41
Nile	Nov./1991	EB	11.75 Inches	202	135
Nile	Sept./1993	RB	2.5 Inches	2,001	12.2
Nile	Oct./1994	RB	2.75 Inches	4,037	34.5

Lake	Date	Species	Avg. Size	Number	Pounds
Rigley	April/1989	RB	14.5 Inches	120	158
Rigley	April/1989	RB	10 Inches	533	205
Rigley	April/1990	RB	16 Inches	100	160
Rigley	April/1990	RB	10 Inches	500	200
Rigley	April/1991	RB	16.5 Inches	100	185
Rigley	April/1991	RB	9.75 Inches	527	195
Rigley	April/1992	RB	16.5 Inches	100	180
Rigley	April/1992	RB	9 Inches	502	152
Rigley	April/1993	RB	8 Inches	500	100
Rigley	April/1993	RB	5.75 Pounds	150	855
Rigley	April/1994	RB	7.5 Inches	501	88
Rigley	May/1994	RB	5.6 Pounds	100	560
Rigley	May/1994	RB	16 Inches	100	170
Cedar	May/1989	RB	3.5 Inches	11,514	202
Cedar	May/1989	RB	3.25 Inches	11,492	169
Cedar	May/1990	RB	3.25 Inches	11,040	160
Cedar	May/1990	RB	3.25 Inches	8,960	128
Cedar	May/1991	RB	3.25 Inches	20,025	267
Cedar	May/1992	RB	3.5 Inches	19,971	317
Cedar	May/1993	RB	3.25 Inches	19,992	294
Cedar	May/1994	RB	3.5 Inches	4,981	84
Cedar	May/1994	RB	3.5 Inches	15,048	264
Rocky	May/1989	RB	3 Inches	5,963	67
Rocky	April/1990	RB	3.25 Inches	6,164	92
Rocky	May/1991	RB	3 Inches	5,986	73
Rocky	May/1992	RB	3.5 Inches	7,015	115
Rocky	May/1993	RB	3.25 Inches	7,008	96
Rocky	May/1994	RB	3.5 Inches	7,020	108
McDowell	April/1989	RB	3 Inches	2,009	20.5
McDowell	May/1989	RB	8.75 Inches	2,016	545
McDowell	May/1989	RB	15.5 Inches	200	320
McDowell	May/1991	AG	3.25 Inches	443	5.8
McDowell	Nov./1992	BT	2.5 Pounds	200	500
McDowell	April/1994	RB	7.5 Inches	501	88
McDowell	April/1994	RB	16 Inches	100	180
Starvation	May/1989	RB	3 Inches	18,067	203
Starvation	April/1990	RB	3.25 Inches	9,648	144
Starvation	April/1990	RB	3.25 Inches	8,325	111
Starvation	May/1991	RB	3.25 Inches	19,988	263
Starvation	May/1992	RB	3.5 Inches	20,007	351
Starvation	April/1993	RB	3.25 Inches	20,007	247
Starvation	April/1993	RB	8 Inches	5,000	1,000
Starvation	April/1993	RB	5.75 Pounds	275	1,568
Starvation	May/1994	RB	3.5 Inches	9,360	144
Starvation	May/1994	RB	3.5 Inches	10,720	160
Bayley	June/1989	EB	3 Inches	516	6
Bayley	May/1990	EB	3.25 Inches	532	7
Bayley	May/1991	EB	3 Inches	504	5.3
Bayley	April/1991	RB	8.25 Inches	495	110
Bayley	April/1992	RB	9 Inches	500	147
Bayley	April/1993	RB	8 Inches	500	100
Bayley	April/1993	RB	5.75 Pounds	100	570
Bayley	April/1994	RB	7.5 Inches	501	88
Long	Sept./1989	WCT	2 Inches	8,000	26
Long	Sept./1990	WCT	2.5 Inches	7,990	47
Long	May/1992	WCT	4.75 Inches	4,592	164
Long	May/1993	WCT	4.75 Inches	7,007	245
Long	Oct./1993	WCT	2.75 Inches	8,232	56
Long	Oct./1994	WCT	2.5 Inches	7,987	49
Curlew	June/1989	EB	4 Inches	1,170	30
Curlew	June/1989	EB	3.25 Inches	25,060	313

Lake	Date	Species	Avg. Size	Number	Pounds
Curlew	June/1989	EB	3 Inches	4,785	55
Curlew	Nov./1989	RB	8.5 Inches	24,730	6,182.5
Curlew	Sept./1989	RB	5.75 Inches	15,600	1,200
Curlew	Sept./1989	RB	5.75 Inches	14,365	1,105
Curlew	Sept./1989	RB	5.75 Inches	16,250	1,300
Curlew	Sept./1989	RB	5.75 Inches	14,690	1,130
Curlew	Sept./1989	RB	5.75 Inches	16,705	1,285
Curlew	Sept./1989	RB	6 Inches	11,716	1,010
Curlew	Sept./1989	RB	6 Inches	10,890	990
Curlew	May/1989	RB	3.25 Inches	50,050	715
Curlew	May/1989	RB	3.25 Inches	50,040	695
Curlew	Aug./1989	RB	5.25 Inches	16,380	910
Curlew	July/1990	RB	5 Inches	49,880	2,625
Curlew	Aug./1990	RB	5.75 Inches	12,710	1,025
Curlew	Aug./1990	RB	5.75 Inches	16,302	1,235
Curlew	Aug./1990	RB	5.75 Inches	14,605	1,150
Curlew	Aug./1990	RB	5.75 Inches	19,328	1,510
Curlew	Aug./1990	RB	5.75 Inches	9,928	730
Curlew	Sept./1990	RB	5.5 Inches	15,803	1,075
Curlew	Sept./1990	RB	5.25 Inches	18,000	1,000
Curlew	Sept./1990	RB	5.25 Inches	15,770	950
Curlew	Sept./1990	RB	5.25 Inches	14,960	900
Curlew	Sept./1990	RB	5.25 Inches	12,760	755
Curlew	April/1991	EB	2.5 Inches	59,943	377
Curlew	Sept./1991	RB	5.5 Inches	63,492	4,070
Curlew	Sept./1991	RB	5.5 Inches	62,040	4,400
Curlew	Sept./1992	RB	5.25 Inches	81,000	5,000
Curlew	Sept./1992	RB	5.25 Inches	68,992	3,920
Curlew	Oct./1993	RB	6 Inches	10,800	900
Curlew	Oct./1993	RB	5.75 Inches	65,000	5,000
Curlew	Oct./1993	RB	5.75 Inches	8,684	668
Curlew	Oct./1993	RB	5.75 Inches	65,529	4,927
Curlew	Oct./1994	RB	6 Inches	14,973	1,225
Curlew	Oct./1994	RB	6 Inches	14,945	1,215
Curlew	Oct./1994	RB	5.75 Inches	16,796	1,235
Curlew	Oct./1994	RB	5.25 Inches	19,800	1,200
Curlew	Oct./1994	RB	5.5 Inches	17,360	1,240
Curlew	Oct./1994	RB	5.5 Inches	17,444	1,203
Curlew	Oct./1994	RB	6 Inches	16,320	1,360
Curlew	Oct./1994	RB	6 Inches	16,320	1,360
Curlew	Oct./1994	RB	5.75 Inches	15,405	1,213

REGION 2

Lake	Date	Species	Avg. Size	Number	Pounds
Chopaka	May/1990	RB	3.25 Inches	6,000	75
Chopaka	May/1991	RB	3.25 Inches	4,550	65
Chopaka	May/1992	RB	3 Inches	5,046	58
Chopaka	May/1993	RB	3 Inches	4,050	45
Chopaka	May/1994	RB	2.5 Inches	4,500	25
Sidley	Oct./1989	LCT	3.25 Inches	5,025	67
Sidley	May/1989	RB	3.25 Inches	25,040	313
Sidley	May/1990	RB	3.25 Inches	20,000	250
Sidley	May/1991	RB	3.25 Inches	20,020	286
Sidley	May/1992	RB	3 Inches	20,010	230
Sidley	May/1993	RB	3 Inches	20,072	208
Sidley	May/1994	RB	2.5 Inches	4,680	26
Sidley	May/1994	RB	2.5 Inches	5,480	40
Proctor	May/1989	EB	2.75 Inches	1,026	9
Proctor	May/1990	RB	3.25 Inches	1,050	15
Proctor	May/1991	RB	3.25 Inches	1,260	18
Proctor	May/1992	RB	3 Inches	1,566	18

Lake	Date	Species	Avg. Size	Number	Pounds
Proctor	May/1993	RB	3 Inches	1,500	15
Proctor	May/1994	RB	2.5 Inches	1,080	6
Blue	Sept./1989	LCT	3.25 Inches	2,520	28
Blue	Oct./1990	LCT	4.25 Inches	3,034	82
Blue	Sept./1991	LCT	4.5 Inches	2,520	84
Blue	Oct./1992	LCT	4.5 Inches	2,516	74
Blue	Oct./1993	LCT	4.25 Inches	2,509	65
Blue	Oct./1994	LCT	3.75 Inches	2,548	49
Ell	May/1989	RB	3 Inches	1,218	14
Ell	May/1990	RB	3.25 Inches	1,260	18
Ell	May/1991	RB	3.25 Inches	1,260	18
Ell	May/1992	RB	3.25 Inches	1,248	16
Ell	May/1993	RB	3 Inches	1,242	12
Ell	May/1994	RB	2.5 Inches	1,027	7.5
Big Twin	Oct./1989	LCT	3.25 Inches	5,025	67
Big Twin	May/1989	RB	3 Inches	12,035	145
Big Twin	Oct./1990	LCT	4.25 Inches	4,033	109
Big Twin	May/1990	RB	3 Inches	4,048	44
Big Twin	Sept./1991	LCT	4.5 Inches	2,010	67
Big Twin	May/1991	RB	3.25 Inches	5,025	67
Big Twin	Oct./1992	LCT	4.25 Inches	1,020	30
Big Twin	May/1992	RB	3.5 Inches	4,278	69
Big Twin	Oct./1993	LCT	5 Inches	1,012	44
Big Twin	May/1993	RB	3.25 Inches	2,025	25
Big Twin	May/1994	RB	3.5 Inches	4,004	77
Big Twin	Oct./1994	LCT	3.5 Inches	1,144	22
Blue	May/1989	RB	3 Inches	10,005	115
Blue	May/1990	RB	3.25 Inches	20,000	250
Blue	May/1991	RB	3.25 Inches	25,000	358
Blue	May/1992	RB	3.25 Inches	8,034	103
Blue	May/1993	RB	2.75 Inches	1,044	9
Blue	May/1994	RB	2.5 Inches	3,014	22
Aeneas	May/1989	RB	3.25 Inches	6,000	75
Aeneas	May/1990	RB	3.25 Inches	6,000	75
Aeneas	May/1991	RB	3.25 Inches	6,020	86
Aeneas	May/1992	RB	3.25 Inches	6,006	77
Aeneas	May/1993	RB	3 Inches	5,974	58
Aeneas	May/1994	RB	2.5 Inches	5,040	28
Dry Falls	May/1989	RB	3.25 Inches	13,711	179
Dry Falls	May/1990	BT	3.5 Inches	1,972	34
Dry Falls	May/1990	RB	3 Inches	10,034	116
Dry Falls	May/1991	BT	3.5 Inches	1,989	39
Dry Falls	April/1991	RB	2.75 Inches	10,989	99
Dry Falls	May/1992	BT	3.25 Inches	2,044	28
Dry Falls	May/1992	RB	3.25 Inches	11,023	151
Dry Falls	May/1993	BT	3 Inches	2,012	23.4
Dry Falls	April/1993	RB	3 Inches	11,021	107
Dry Falls	May/1994	RB	3.5 Inches	10,997	171.3
Dry Falls	June/1994	BT	4 Inches	2,000	54.8
Lenore	Sept./1989	LCT	3.25 Inches	50,040	556
Lenore	Oct./1990	LCT	4.25 Inches	40,034	1,082
Lenore	Oct./1991	LCT	4.5 Inches	40,020	1,334
Lenore	Oct./1992	LCT	4.5 Inches	40,018	1,177
Lenore	Oct./1993	LCT	5 Inches	9,200	400
Lenore	Oct./1993	LCT	5 Inches	9,200	400
Lenore	Oct./1993	LCT	5 Inches	23,000	1,000
Lenore	Oct./1993	LCT	5 Inches	23,000	1,000
Lenore	Oct./1993	LCT	5 Inches	7,820	340
Lenore	Oct./1993	LCT	5 Inches	7,820	340
Lenore	Oct./1994	LCT	3.75 Inches	40,040	770
Lenore	Oct./1994	LCT	3.75 Inches	3,850	70

Lake	Date	Species	Avg. Size	Number	Pounds
Jameson	May/1989	RB	3.5 Inches	90,074	1,553
Jameson	May/1989	RB	3.5 Inches	109,312	1,792
Jameson	May/1990	RB	3 Inches	69,276	753
Jameson	April/1990	RB	3 Inches	156,016	1,592
Jameson	April/1991	RB	3 Inches	201,590	2,122
Jameson	May/1992	RB	3 Inches	210,956	2,293
Jameson	April/1993	RB	3 Inches	200,345	2,357
Jameson	April/1993	RB	2.75 Inches	26,250	250
Jameson	May/1994	RB	3.25 Inches	202,048	2,624
Grimes	Sept./1989	LCT	3.25 Inches	8,010	89
Grimes	Oct./1990	LCT	4.25 Inches	8,029	217
Grimes	Sept./1991	LCT	4.5 Inches	8,010	267
Grimes	Oct./1992	LCT	4.5 Inches	8,024	236
Grimes	Oct./1993	LCT	4.25 Inches	8,106	210
Grimes	Oct./1994	LCT	3.75 Inches	8,008	154
Nunnally	April/1989	RB	2.75 Inches	12,992	116
Nunnally	May/1989	BT	3.75 Inches	2,002	44.5
Nunnally	May/1990	BT	3.5 Inches	2,030	35
Nunnally	May/1990	RB	3 Inches	12,975	150
Nunnally	May/1991	BT	3.75 Inches	1,989	39
Nunnally	April/1991	RB	2.75 Inches	12,971	119
Nunnally	May/1992	BT	3.25 Inches	2,000	27.4
Nunnally	May/1992	RB	3 Inches	12,996	152
Nunnally	April/1993	RB	3 Inches	12,986	151
Nunnally	May/1993	BT	3 Inches	1,978	23
Nunnally	May/1994	RB	3.5 Inches	12,985	245
Nunnally	Sept./1994	BT	7 Inches	2,002	282
Merry	April/1989	RB	2.75 Inches	3,024	27
Merry	May/1990	RB	3 Inches	3,028	35
Merry	May/1991	RB	3.25 Inches	2,993	41
Merry	May/1992	RB	3 Inches	2,992	35
Merry	April/1993	RB	3 Inches	3,010	35
Merry	May/1994	RB	3.25 Inches	2,996	45.4
Lenice	May/1989	BT	3.75 Inches	2,002	44.5
Lenice	April/1989	RB	2.75 Inches	8,960	80
Lenice	May/1990	BT	3.5 Inches	1,972	34
Lenice	May/1990	RB	3 Inches	8,996	104
Lenice	May/1991	BT	3.5 Inches	1,989	39
Lenice	May/1991	RB	3.25 Inches	8,979	123
Lenice	May/1992	BT	3.25 Inches	1,314	18
Lenice	May/1992	RB	3 Inches	8,977	105
Lenice	May/1993	BT	3 Inches	1,978	23
Lenice	April/1993	RB	3 Inches	9,030	105
Lenice	May/1994	RB	3.25 Inches	9,009	136.5
Lenice	Sept./1994	BT	7 Inches	2,002	282
Quail	Feb./1990	RB	10 Inches	1,250	500
Quail	Feb./1990	RB	10 Inches	1,250	500
Quail	May/1991	BT	3.5 Inches	510	10
Quail	May/1991	RB	3.25 Inches	1,022	14
Quail	April/1992	BT	3.25 Inches	499	6.8
Quail	April/1992	RB	3 Inches	1,020	12
Quail	April/1993	RB	3.25 Inches	1,020	13
Quail	May/1993	BT	3 Inches	516	6
Quail	April/1994	RB	3.25 Inches	1,000	12.5
Quail	June/1994	BT	4 Inches	500	13.7

REGION 3

Lake	Date	Species	Avg. Size	Number	Pounds
Wenas	May/1989	BT	3.75 Inches	11,000	220
Wenas	May/1989	RB	3.25 Inches	29,944	394
Wenas	March/1989	RB	8 Inches	5,000	1,000

Lake	Date	Species	Avg. Size	Number	Pounds
Wenas	March/1989	RB	8 Inches	5,000	1,000
Wenas	March/1989	RB	8 Inches	5,000	1,000
Wenas	May/1989	RB	3.5 Inches	6,999	2,333
Wenas	Nov./1989	RB	6.75 Inches	7,030	925
Wenas	May/1990	BT	3.5 Inches	12,996	228
Wenas	Oct./1990	BT	7 Inches	2,996	428
Wenas	March/1990	RB	8.25 Inches	4,950	1,100
Wenas	March/1990	RB	7.75 Inches	853	147
Wenas	April/1990	RB	8.25 Inches	6,795	1,510
Wenas	May/1990	RB	8.25 Inches	4,500	1,000
Wenas	Oct./1990	RB	6.75 Inches	8,257	1,007
Wenas	June/1991	BT	3.75 Inches	10,998	234
Wenas	Oct./1991	BT	8 Inches	1,944	405
Wenas	March/1991	RB	8.5 Inches	3,822	910
Wenas	March/1991	RB	8.5 Inches	3,402	810
Wenas	April/1991	RB	9.5 Inches	8,000	2,857
Wenas	May/1991	RB	9.25 Inches	2,512	785
Wenas	May/1991	RB	9.25 Inches	2,912	910
Wenas	June/1991	RB	2.75 Inches	25,088	224
Wenas	June/1991	RB	9.5 Inches	3,640	1,255
Wenas	Nov./1991	RB	7.5 Inches	5,040	840
Wenas	Dec./1991	RB	7 Inches	4,060	580
Wenas	June/1992	BT	4 Inches	11,040	276
Wenas	Oct./1992	BT	8.75 Inches	4,028	1,060
Wenas	March/1992	RB	8.5 Inches	4,520	1,130
Wenas	March/1992	RB	8.5 Inches	4,460	1,115
Wenas	April/1992	RB	8.5 Inches	9,440	2,360
Wenas	April/1992	RB	8.5 Inches	1,544	386
Wenas	May/1992	RB	9 Inches	3,933	1,210
Wenas	May/1992	RB	9 Inches	3,944	1,195
Wenas	June/1992	RB	9.5 Inches	2,640	880
Wenas	June/1992	RB	9.5 Inches	2,505	835
Wenas	June/1992	RB	3.75 Inches	30,444	590
Wenas	Nov./1992	RB	7.25 Inches	4,505	715
Wenas	May/1993	BT	3.25 Inches	11,016	162
Wenas	Oct./1993	BT	8.5 Inches	2,847	730
Wenas	Oct./1993	BT	8.5 Inches	2,920	730
Wenas	Feb./1993	RB	9 Inches	7,088	2,025
Wenas	March/1993	RB	8.5 Inches	3,213	765
Wenas	April/1993	RB	9.25 Inches	1,550	500
Wenas	April/1993	RB	8 Inches	2,424	505
Wenas	April/1993	RB	9.25 Inches	3,550	1,145
Wenas	April/1993	RB	9.25 Inches	1,581	510
Wenas	May/1993	RB	9.5 Inches	1,320	455
Wenas	May/1993	RB	9.5 Inches	1,260	420
Wenas	May/1993	RB	9.5 Inches	2,430	810
Wenas	June/1993	RB	3.25 Inches	30,044	370
Wenas	June/1993	RB	9.5 Inches	2,580	860
Wenas	June/1993	RB	9.5 Inches	2,460	820
Wenas	March/1994	RB	8 Inches	5,000	1,000
Wenas	March/1994	RB	8 Inches	2,025	405
Wenas	April/1994	RB	8.5 Inches	984	240
Wenas	April/1994	RB	8.5 Inches	4,924	1,201
Wenas	May/1994	BT	3.5 Inches	11,136	174
Wenas	May/1994	BT	8.75 Inches	4,015	1,085
Wenas	June/1994	RB	3 Inches	19,980	222
Wenas	June/1994	RB	9.5 Inches	3,683	1,270
Wenas	Sept./1994	BT	8 Inches	3,240	675
Wenas	Oct./1994	RB	8 Inches	1,000	200

REGION 4

Lake	Date	Species	Avg. Size	Number	Pounds
Pass	Feb./1989	CCT	6.5 Inches	5,000	500
Pass	May/1989	RB	4.5 Inches	10,065	366
Pass	July/1989	AT	7.75 Inches	1,352	265
Pass	Oct./1989	BT	6.25 Inches	5,000	500
Pass	Feb./1990	CCT	7.75 Inches	4,960	800
Pass	May/1990	RB	4.5 Inches	10,080	360
Pass	Oct./1990	CCT	4.5 Inches	4,050	135
Pass	May/1991	RB	4.5 Inches	8,083	295
Pass	May/1991	AT	5.5 Inches	6,083	441
Pass	Dec./1991	CCT	6 Inches	5,040	360
Pass	May/1992	RB	3.75 Inches	10,125	225
Pass	June/1992	CCT	2.25 Inches	5,103	21
Pass	Oct./1992	RB	1.75 Inches	14,080	32
Pass	Oct./1992	BT	6.5 Inches	5,029	535
Pass	May/1993	CCT	2 Inches	4,760	14
Pass	May/1993	RB	4.25 Inches	10,131	330
Pass	Oct./1993	BT	6 Inches	3,575	325
Pass	May/1994	RB	4.75 Inches	10,125	450
Pass	Nov./1994	BT	6 Inches	3,000	275
Squalicum	Oct./1989	CCT	4 Inches	2,065	51
Squalicum	Aug./1990	CCT	3.5 Inches	2,138	34
Ebey	Oct./1990	CCT	3.25 Inches	2,064	24
Ebey	June/1991	CCT	2.25 Inches	2,070	9
Ebey	Sept./1992	CCT	2.75 Inches	1,020	8.5
Ebey	Sept./1993	CCT	3.25 Inches	1,012	13.5
Ebey	Sept./1993	RB	4.75 Inches	1,000	42
Ebey	Sept./1994	CCT	3.5 Inches	986	17
Lone	March/1989	RB	8.25 Inches	7,568	1,720
Lone	May/1989	RB	3.25 Inches	25,050	334
Lone	April/1990	RB	8.5 Inches	5,187	1,235
Lone	April/1990	RB	8.5 Inches	2,331	555
Lone	May/1990	RB	3 Inches	30,295	365
Lone	March/1991	RB	8.5 Inches	7,544	1,840
Lone	April/1991	RB	8.25 Inches	3,555	790
Lone	May/1991	RB	3.25 Inches	29,796	382
Lone	April/1992	RB	8.5 Inches	3,948	940
Lone	June/1992	RB	3 Inches	30,195	305
Lone	April/1993	RB	8 Inches	4,368	840
Lone	June/1993	RB	2.75 Inches	30,030	273
Lone	April/1994	RB	9 Inches	1,750	500
Lone	May/1994	RB	8.25 Inches	2,115	470
Lone	May/1994	RB	3 Inches	30,000	300
Rattlesnake	March/1989	RB	8.25 Inches	8,032	1,868
Rattlesnake	March/1989	RB	8.25 Inches	9,147	2,079
Rattlesnake	March/1989	RB	8.5 Inches	5,684	1,421
Rattlesnake	May/1989	RB	10.75 Inches	3,800	1,900
Rattlesnake	May/1989	RB	2.75 Inches	12,600	120
Rattlesnake	Oct./1989	RB	5.5 Inches	5,505	367
Rattlesnake	March/1990	RB	9.25 Inches	5,385	1,795
Rattlesnake	March/1990	RB	8.75 Inches	5,502	1,448
Rattlesnake	April/1990	RB	10.75 Inches	3,000	1,500
Rattlesnake	May/1990	RB	2.75 Inches	11,970	114
Rattlesnake	March/1991	RB	8.25 Inches	2,875	625
Rattlesnake	March/1991	RB	7.75 Inches	10,853	1,938
Rattlesnake	April/1991	RB	8.25 Inches	4,002	870
Rattlesnake	May/1991	RB	3 Inches	11,970	126
Rattlesnake	Nov./1991	RB	2.25 Pounds	100	225
Rattlesnake	Nov./1991	RB	5.5 Pounds	50	276

Lake	Date	Species	Avg. Size	Number	Pounds
Rattlesnake	April/1992	RB	10.75 Inches	980	490
Rattlesnake	May/1992	RB	3 Inches	12,000	120
Rattlesnake	April/1993	RB	9.75 Inches	637	245
Rattlesnake	April/1993	RB	9 Inches	1,558	445
Rattlesnake	April/1993	RB	8.25 Inches	10,418	2,315
Rattlesnake	May/1993	RB	8.75 Inches	1,602	445
Rattlesnake	May/1993	RB	2.75 Inches	12,000	104.3
Rattlesnake	March/1994	RB	11 Inches	750	375
Rattlesnake	April/1994	RB	8.5 Inches	10,000	2,500
Rattlesnake	May/1994	RB	3 Inches	11,970	126

REGION 5

Lake	Date	Species	Avg. Size	Number	Pounds
Coldwater	Aug./1989	RB	5.75 Inches	10,050	750
Coldwater	Aug./1989	RB	6 Inches	9,860	850
Coldwater	Sept./1989	RB	6 Inches	10,502	890
Merrill	April/1989	RB	9.5 Inches	3,480	1,200
Merrill	April/1989	RB	8.5 Inches	4,680	1,200
Merrill	April/1989	RB	8.5 Inches	4,641	1,190
Merrill	July/1989	BT	4.5 Inches	13,050	450
Merrill	July/1989	BT	5.25 Inches	12,085	664
Merrill	April/1990	BT	9 Inches	3,960	1,200
Merrill	April/1990	RB	9 Inches	4,097	1,205
Merrill	May/1990	BT	9 Inches	3,927	1,190
Merrill	May/1990	BT	9 Inches	3,498	1,060
Merrill	June/1990	RB	11.75 Inches	1,650	1,100
Merrill	Aug./1990	BT	4.5 Inches	15,002	577
Merrill	April/1991	BT	8.5 Inches	6,020	1,505
Merrill	May/1991	BT	8.75 Inches	2,556	710
Merrill	June/1991	BT	3.25 Inches	25,000	312
Merrill	Sept./1991	BT	6.25 Inches	4,998	490
Merrill	July/1992	BT	5 Inches	25,016	1,180
Merrill	March/1993	BT	8 Inches	4,484	915
Merrill	March/1993	BT	8 Inches	4,410	900
Merrill	Aug./1993	BT	4 Inches	25,500	600
Merrill	May/1994	BT	7.75 Inches	3,975	750
Merrill	May/1994	BT	8.25 Inches	3,118	725
Merrill	August/1994	BT	5 Inches	25,000	1,250

REGION 6

Lake	Date	Species	Avg. Size	Number	Pounds
Anderson	June/1989	EB	2 Inches	7,700	25
Anderson	June/1989	RB	3 Inches	24,840	270
Anderson	March/1990	RB	8.25 Inches	5,016	1,140
Anderson	May/1990	RB	9 Inches	4,270	1,220
Anderson	May/1990	RB	2.75 Inches	30,420	260
Anderson	June/1990	EB	2 Inches	7,013	25.5
Anderson	June/1990	EB	7.5 Inches	5,502	917
Anderson	June/1991	RB	2.75 Inches	30,210	285
Anderson	May/1992	RB	8.75 Inches	5,994	1,620
Anderson	June/1992	RB	3 Inches	29,963	361
Anderson	May/1993	CCT	6.75 Inches	10,710	1,260
Anderson	June/1993	RB	2.5 Inches	29,920	176
Anderson	May/1994	RB	8.5 Inches	3,620	905
Anderson	June/1994	RB	3 Inches	29,925	285
Buck	May/1989	RB	7.75 Inches	1,802	340
Buck	June/1989	RB	3 Inches	7,995	97.5
Buck	April/1990	RB	8.25 Inches	1,320	300
Buck	May/1990	RB	8 Inches	1,450	290
Buck	June/1990	CCT	2 Inches	1,050	3
Buck	June/1990	EB	7.5 Inches	498	83

Lake	Date	Species	Avg. Size	Number	Pounds
Buck	June/1990	RB	3.25 Inches	5,025	67
Buck	March/1991	RB	8 Inches	2,550	510
Buck	May/1991	RB	8.5 Inches	1,200	300
Buck	May/1991	RB	3 Inches	8,010	90
Buck	April/1992	RB	8.25 Inches	2,021	470
Buck	May/1992	RB	8.75 Inches	999	270
Buck	Dec./1992	RB	7.25 Inches	1,504	235
Buck	May/1993	RB	2.25 Inches	9,984	52
Buck	May/1994	RB	8.5 Inches	1,025	250
Buck	May/1994	RB	3 Inches	14,839	162
Prices	June/1989	CCT	2 Inches	2,002	6.5
Prices	June/1989	EB	2 Inches	1,006	3.7
Prices	June/1989	RB	3.25 Inches	2,508	33
Prices	May/1991	RB	3.25 Inches	2,025	27
Prices	July/1992	CCT	2.25 Inches	1,972	8.5
Prices	July/1992	EB	3 Inches	998	10.5
Prices	July/1992	RB	3.5 Inches	1,020	17

Appendix B
Transportation Information

To receive the free Official Washington State Highway Map call the Department of Transportation at (360) 357-2600 or write: Washington State Department of Transportation; 5720 Capitol Boulevard, Tumwater 7440; Olympia, WA 98504-7440. The map has an excellent, detailed mileage table that is very useful.

Toll free schedule information for the Washington State Ferries is available by calling 1-800-84-FERRY. For more information, write Washington State Ferries; Colman Dock/Pier 52; 801 Alaskan Way; Seattle, WA 98104-1487.

To request information on Washington State Parks, call (206) 753-2027. You may also write: Washington State Parks; 7150 Cleanwater Lane; P.O. Box 42650; Olympia, WA 98504-2650.

Appendix C
Washington Department of Fish and Wildlife Information

To receive the Fishing Regulations Pamphlet or other management information, please contact the Washington Department of Fish and Wildlife at:

Olympia Office
600 Capitol Way North
Olympia, WA 98501-1091
(360) 902-2200

Wenatchee Office
3860 Chelan Hwy. North
Wenatchee, WA 98801-9607
(509) 662-0452

Region 1
8702 North Division St.
Spokane, WA 99218-1199
(509) 456-4082

Region 4
16018 Mill Creek Blvd.
Mill Creek, WA 98012-1296
(206) 775-1311

Region 2
1550 Alder St. Northwest
Ephrata, WA 98823-9699
(509) 754-4624

Region 5
5405 NE Hazel Dell Avenue
Vancouver, WA 98563
(360) 696-6211

Region 3
1701 South 24th Avenue
Yakima, WA 98902-5720
(509) 575-2740

Region 6
48 Devonshire Road
Montesano, WA 98563
(360) 249-4628

Bibliography

- Most bathymetric maps in this book were prepared 20 or more years ago by the Washington Department of Game and the U.S. Geological Survey. They were obtained from the following Washington State Division of Water Resources and Washington State Department of Ecology publications: *Lakes of Washington* (volumes 1-2), *Data on Selected Lakes in Washington* (Water Supply Bulletin 42, volumes 1-6), and *Reconnaissance Data on Lakes in Washington* (Water Supply Bulletin 43, volumes 1-7). Pass Lake contour map was provided by the Fidalgo Fly Fishers Club. Coldwater Lake contour map was provided by Mount Saint Helens National Volcanic Monument.

- Allen, John Eliot, Marjorie Burns, Sam Sargent. *Cataclysms on the Columbia.* Portland: Timber Press, 1986.

- Battien, Pauline. *The Gold Seekers.* Colville: Pauline Battien, 1989.

- Burgis, Mary and Pat Morris. *The Natural History of Lakes.* Cambridge: Cambridge University Press, 1987.

- Cordes, Ron, and Randall Kaufmann. *Lake Fishing with a Fly.* Portland: Frank Amato Publications, Inc., 1984.

- Cotes, O.J., and Glen Nenema. *The Kalispels, People of the Pend Oreille.* Provided by the Kalispel Tribe of Indians.

- Hughes, Dave. *Strategies for Stillwater.* Harrisburg: Stackpole Books, 1991.

- Johnson, Daniel M. *Atlas of Oregon Lakes.* Corvallis: Oregon State University Press, 1985.

- Kirk, Ruth, and Carmela Alexander. *Exploring Washington's Past.* Seattle: University of Washington Press, 1990.

- Molson-Chesaw-Knob Hill Community Development Committee. *Okanogan Highland Album.* Colville: Molson-Chesaw-Knob Hill Community Development Committee, 1987.

- Molson-Chesaw-Knob Hill Community Development Committee. *Okanogan Highland Echoes.* Colville: Molson-Chesaw-Knob Hill Community Development Committee, 1962.

- Raymond, Steve. *Kamloops.* Portland: Frank Amato Publications, Inc., 1980, 1994.

- Waring, Guy. *My Pioneer Past.* Boston: B. Humphries, 1936.

- Weis, Paul, and William Newman. *The Channeled Scablands of Eastern Washington.* Cheney: Eastern Washington University Press, 1989.

- Welch, Paul. *Liminology.* New York: McGraw-Hill Book Company, 1935.

- Wetzel, Robert G. *Limnology.* Philadelphia: Saunders, 1983.

Medical Lake (page 24).

Amber Lake (page 28).

Browns Lake (page 31).

Nile Lake (page 35).

Rigley Lake (page 38).

Cedar Lake (page 41).

Rocky Lake (page 43).

McDowell Lake (page 46).

Starvation Lake (page 50).

Bayley Lake (page 52).

Curlew Lake (page 59).

Chopaka Lake (page 64).

Ell Lake (page 80).

Big Twin Lake (page 83).

Aeneas Lake (page 90).

Dry Falls Lake (page 93).

Lenore Lake (page 98).

Jameson Lake (page 101).

Grimes Lake (page 104).

Merry Lake (page 110).

Quail Lake (page 115).

Squalicum Lake (page 128).

Ebey Lake (page 130).

Lone Lake (page 133).

Rattlesnake Lake (page 135).

Coldwater Lake (page 140).

Merrill Lake (page 143).

Anderson Lake (page 148).

Prices Lake (page 154).

Sunrise reflected in the icy waters on a high mountain lake.

Sheer beauty surrounds the high mountain lakes.